NATIVE AMERICAN
FAQs HANDBOOK

BY GEORGE RUSSELL
SAGINAW CHIPPEWA

Russell Publications
9027 N. Cobre Drive
Phoenix, AZ 85028
Phone: (800) 835-7220
Email: russell@nativeamericanonline.com

Cover and book design:
Masterpiece Publishing, LLC
Michele O'Hagan
(602) 866-3226

The *Native American FAQs Handbook* is a revised edition of
the *American Indian Digest* (1993, 1995) and the
American Indian Facts of Life (1997) written and published
by George Russell of Russell Publications.

Native American FAQs Handbook
ISBN: 1- 881933-10-5
Copyright © 2000
All rights reserved.
Printed in the USA

The *Native American FAQs Handbook*
complements the Native American Reservations map
and the Native American Online portal at
www.nativeamericanonline.com

Acknowledgement

Serenity Prayer

Lord, grant me the serenity,
To accept the things I cannot change,
The courage, commitment and character,
To change the things I can,
And the wisdom to know the difference.
— Anonymous

Mary Ganton

I met Mary Ganton, when I was about 9 years old, shortly after we had left the reservation and moved to the small farming community of Dansville, Michigan. We attended the Free Methodist Church and Mary was my first Sunday School teacher.

She was a devoted mother to her own four sons and still found time to be a surrogate mother to other needy souls in the community, including myself. After her sons were grown, she adopted four more young children, including a 2 week-old infant, who are now grown.

Mary lives in Spring Arbor, Michigan where she continues to be a Christian witness and pillar in her community. Her love and support has been inspirational to all who know her and I want to express my heartfelt gratitude to a remarkable woman for her constant presence and profound influence in my life.

As we begin a new millennium,
we can only wonder what the Native
American experience will be 100 years
from now. The world is moving at
"Internet speed" and concern with
Native American issues will diminish
in direct proportion to the speed of
change. Congress simply does not
have the time, information or
inclination to deal with Native
American issues.

Foreword

The purpose of this handbook is to provide information about today's Native American population, tribes and reservations.

"For a subject that has been worked and reworked so often in novels, motion pictures and television, American Indians are the least understood and the most misunderstood Americans of us all."
— President John F. Kennedy, 1963

Mission Statement

The purpose of this handbook is to provide information about today's Native American population, tribes and reservations.

Vision Statement

This Native American FAQ's Handbook is part of a three-part package. By the time you read this handbook, our newest map, "Native American Reservations" will be in print. The Native American Online (www.nativeamericanonline.com) portal is up and running and will continue to be a work in progress. Native American Online will become the main source of information because it can be updated and accessed quickly.

The vision is for Native American Online to be a network of every tribal website in the country. We will link to the existing tribal websites and build websites for the smaller tribes that do not have the resources or expertise.

The history of the Native people of this country is a vast, complex and diverse subject that would take a lifetime of study to understand. The goal of Native American FAQ's is to present enough information, direction and reference to motivate the reader to do further study and research in their area of interest.

Libraries, universities and museums contain thousands of voluminous resources that chronicle every aspect of the fascinating epic as two conflicting cultures engaged in a violent and savage struggle for survival. For Native Americans the struggle continues.

Book format

For this 6th edition of this handbook, we will use the FAQ's format. During presentations, my favorite time is the question and answer sessions. The exchange of information and ideas is much more interesting than delivering information. FAQ's may be as close as we can get to that exchange in writing.

Research reference

A few years ago, the research for the map and book was compiled mostly from public libraries, museum libraries and agency reports. One of our basic demographic sources was the 1990 Census.

We are working closely with Census 2000 on a Regional, State and City level and look forward to the final statistics with great anticipation. However, the final stats will not be available for at least another year as of this printing. When those numbers are available, they will be posted or linked to the (*www.nativeamerican-online.com*) portal.

Most of the original research reports and lists are no longer available in print. Most of the revisions and updated information for this printing are compiled from Internet websites. The Internet gives us instant access to a huge amounts of information that pours in faster than it can be assimilated. It's like trying to drink from a fire hose. Whenever possible, we have linked to sites than enhance or contain information that we feel is relative. (See the Bibliography for listings.)

Native People semantics

Native people seem to be going through the same semantic evolution experienced by other ethnic groups. Black people have become African-Americans. Mexicans and Latin people have become Hispanic. Chinese, Koreans, Vietnamese, etc. have become Asians. How important is it to agree on a common collective name? If Native people can't agree on what to call themselves,

The Internet gives us instant access to a huge amount of information that pours in faster than it can be assimilated. It's like trying to drink from a fire hose.

If Native people can't agree on what to call themselves, how much of an impact does it have on collective efforts to address social, political and economic issues?

how much of an impact does it have on collective efforts to address social, political and economic issues?

In 1997, the 5th printing of this handbook was titled: *American Indian – Facts of Life*.

A statement in Chapter 1:

> *For our purposes, we will use "American Indian" and "Indian" designations interchangeably and leave the politically correct semantics to the academic community and future generations.*

Since that time, my thinking about "Indian" and "American Indian" has changed for 3 reasons:

First, "Indians" was a misnomer that we've accepted for 500 years. Columbus thought he had landed in the East Indies and called the natives "Indians." The name "Indian" rightfully belongs to the people of India and the East Indies.

Secondly, a looming issue is confusion and conflict on the Internet. When I do a search for "Indian" or "American Indian," the majority of the listings are related to people from India, their organizations and businesses.

Thirdly, "Native American" has gained acceptance in the academic community and seems to be preferred by the younger generations.

The term "Native American" came into usage in the 1960's to denote the groups served by the Bureau of Indian Affairs: American Indians and Alaska Natives (Indians, Eskimos and Aleuts of Alaska). The Eskimos and Aleuts in Alaska are two culturally distinct groups and are sensitive about being included under the "Indian" designation. They prefer, "Alaska Native." Later the term also included Native Hawaiians and Pacific Islanders in some Federal programs.

As we begin the new millennium, it will be a challenge is to accept "Native American" because "Indian" and "American Indian" is indelibly etched in the subconscious of America and most Native People.

Consequently, the 2000 book printing is titled: *Native American FAQ's.* "Indians" and "American Indians" will be replaced with "Native Americans," "Native Tribes" or "Native People." The thought behind "Native People" is that most tribes had names that referred to themselves as "the people" in their own language.

Indian, American Indian or Native American?

It would be beneficial to agree on a common name and eliminate one basic issue of confusion for non-Natives.

When we left the reservation and people asked about my nationality, I simply said: "I'm a Saginaw Chippewa Indian." There is a difference between being "an Indian" and being "Indian." Being "an Indian" was grammatically correct and definitive with regard to blood quantum and tribal affiliation. Being "Indian" is a mindset and a state of being. I was born "Indian" and I believe that I will always be "Indian" to myself.

Around 1990, I became involved in Native American organizations and activities and made the transition from "Indian" to "American Indian." It wasn't that much of a stretch and I made the change without much difficulty. Becoming a Native American is going to be more of a challenge because it's new and sounds strange.

We will keep "Indian" or "American Indian" where it's institutionalized by the United States government definitions such as the Bureau of Indian Affairs, the Indian Health Service, etc. Although "Native American" sounds awkward in some instances, lets see how it plays.

Author disclaimer

I have lived long enough as an "Indian" to be considered an "elder" and have some sense of historical perspective. Most of my

The thought behind "Native People" is that most tribes had names that referred to themselves as "the people" in their own language.

I owe allegiance to no one except the Native American People.

life has been off-reservation and my occupation as a design engineer and construction contractor has developed some basic common sense. I am not controlled by any agency and the views expressed are my own. I owe allegiance to no one except the Native American People.

Some of the questions and answers are quoted or paraphrased from the Bureau of Indian Affairs (BIA) and other sources. In order to address divisive issues and be fair, it is necessary to state their position and purpose in their own words.

Global perspective

As we begin a new millennium, we can only wonder what the Native American experience will be 100 years from now. The world is moving at "Internet speed" and concern with Native American issues will diminish in direct proportion to the speed of change. Congress simply does not have the time, information or inclination to deal with Native American issues.

Star Trek and space shuttles have let us peek into the foreseeable future as scientists systematically explore the galaxy. What they find will affect the life of every person on this planet. NASA space programs are already busy designing space stations. Are other planets inhabitable? Is there intelligent life on these planets? What effect will these answers have on our religious beliefs? It is presumptuous and arrogant for us to assume that we are the only intelligent life in a universe that, as Carl Sagan succinctly reminded us, has "billions and billions" of planets.

Space explorations are the launching pads for a quantum leap in global perception and evolution. We've seen the space photos of Earth that looks like a giant blue and white marble suspended in space. The moon has changed from a globe of romantic mystique to dusty volcanoes and static human voices. The stars have changed from twinkling points of light to planets ringed by colorful planes of dust and matter.

Computers, the Internet and cost-effective wireless telecommunications have transformed our world into a global community and a global market. Competitive participation is mandatory in the global market for national economic survival. Business is conducted internationally almost as easily as domestic transactions. Internet email gives us access to instant communication with anyone in the world for the price of our local phone service.

A good indicator of the global market impact is the implementation of the metric system in the United States. The United States has been flirting with the metric system for the last 30 years and is the only industrialized nation in the world not on the metric system. The metric system is now mandated by specifications for participation in government contracts.

Technology and especially the internet, is the power behind the electronic bullet train of change. The existing gap between Native Americans and the rest of society widens in direct proportion to the speed of change.

Color of racism

As man adapted to his geographic environment, he developed certain physical characteristics, learned to walk upright, lost some body hair, and became a social creature. Tribalism became a human instinct, based on fear, which was essential for survival. Racism is a mutation of tribalism that evolved from fear to hate. Tribalism to the extreme festers into racism. Racism is learned and generational. Most people still have some degree of tribalism for the simple reason that they are most comfortable around people like themselves.

Racism is socially archaic, maliciously ignorant, and non-productive. It becomes an insidious emotional cancer that leaves the carrier mentally stunted. Mental evolution has simply not kept pace with social evolution. In today's society, human similarities are more important than racial differences.

> *The existing gap between Native Americans and the rest of society widens in direct proportion to the speed of change.*

Racism is learned and generational. Most people still have some degree of tribalism for the simple reason that they are most comfortable around people like themselves.

Within the next couple of generations, racism as we know it will be a moot issue, a done deal. Even hard-core racist need only look at their grandchildren. Racism is a waste of time on a foregone conclusion. Each race must come to terms with its vested interest in other races and lay the issue to rest.

The ideals of democracy are a tribute to man's conceptual humanity. Only human nature stands in the way. It is neither rational nor moral for those who enjoy the tenets of democracy, to deny those same basic rights to others because of their difference in appearance or ideology.

An American paradox: on one hand, racial diversity is one source of the nation's strength; and on the other, it's the source of some of its worst social problems. Like it or not, racial diversity is an inherent component of American society, and America is an inherent component of a global community.

Through DNA genetic testing, we are discovering that historically, racial blood mixing was more prevalent and widespread than anyone realized. When the "nature of the beast" is factored in the equation, who can say with absolute confidence that they know the race of every ancestor for 500 years?

Research evidence indicates that Thomas Jefferson had a long-term relationship with his slave Sally Hemings and probably fathered one or more of her children. This relationship was portrayed as a consensual but it has always been common knowledge that female slaves were often rape victims or mistresses of White plantation owners or overseers. The genetic pyramid created by bi-racial pairing over the generations is enormous. (We need some bright university students to create a genetic model.)

For years, Howard University has used genetic data to study diseases that afflict African-Americans. A side benefit is that genetic testing can be used to help African-Americans discover their ancestral origins in Africa and in America.

African-Americans, who descended from people brought to America as slaves for 350 years, are not so African anymore. The tests have revealed that most African-Americans, no matter how dark their complexion, can claim at least one White or American Indian ancestor.

(Wouldn't it be funny if David Duke, or some of those other KKK Neanderthal idiots, took a DNA test and discovered that perhaps their ancestral bloodlines were not as pure as they thought!)

America must resolve the issues of domestic racism before undertaking the problems of a multi-cultural global market. There are six billion people on this tiny planet and America's 278 million people are only 5% of the world market. America cannot afford racism.

If human development is viewed from a telescopic galaxy perspective, racism becomes insignificant. The further removed from the situation, the less important it becomes. Americans have more pressing matters to deal with than the blood composition or the skin pigmentation of their neighbors.

Native Americans come in all flavors, from vanilla to chocolate and everything in between. From blue-eyed blondes to buffalo soldiers. The racial lines have blurred over the generations. The blending is accelerated by mobility and changes in social attitudes.

The beauty and abundance of multi-racial people erases much of the bigotry.

Native Americans need to be conscious and wary of practicing insidious racism. Dissension and prejudice permeate nearly every aspect of Native American life. It is ironic that some Native Americans practice a kind of racism they endured for hundreds of years. A racism that nearly exterminated the Native people. A kind of tribal racism has kept the Native tribes divided, vulnerable and manageable.

Wouldn't it be funny if David Duke, or some of those other KKK Neanderthal idiots, took a DNA test and discovered that perhaps their ancestral bloodlines were not as pure as they thought!

Notes:

_____

_____

_____

_____

_____

_____

_____

_____

_____

_____

_____

_____

_____

"Before we can set out on the road to success, we have to know where we are going, and before we can know that — we must determine where we have been in the past. It seems a basic requirement to study the history of our Indian people. America has much to learn about the heritage of our American Indians. Only through this study can we as a nation do what must be done if our treatment of the American Indian is not to be marked down for all time as a national disgrace."

— President John F. Kennedy, 1961

Section 1:

The Past

It seems that Native people have been harmed as much by good intentions as by bad intentions. Although the bad intentions were more direct and brutal, the results are the same.

HISTORICAL SYNOPSIS

Chronology from 1492 to the present

This abbreviated list of historical events significantly influenced the course of Native American destiny and provides a chronological timeline.

1492	Arrival of Columbus to the New World.
1607	Jamestown was founded.
1620	Pilgrims land at Plymouth Rock.
1622	First major Indian retaliation.
1744	The Treaty of Lancaster.
1775	American Revolutionary War begins.
1776	US Declaration of Independence.
1778	First treaty between US & Indians.
1783	American Revolutionary War ends.
1803	US Louisiana purchase for $15 million.
1824	BIA established under Dept. of War.
1830	Indian Removal Act.
1848	First gold strike in California.
1850	U.S. eliminates all foreign land claims.
1854	Indian Appropriation Act.
1861	Civil War begins.
1862	Railroad Act.
1865	Civil War ends.
1868	Fort Laramie peace conference.
1871	Treaties end between US & Indians.
1887	General Allotment Act. (Dawes Act)
1917	U.S. enters World War I.
1919	Treaty of Versailles ends World War II.
1924	Indian Citizenship Act.
1934	Indian Reorganization Act.
1941	U.S. enter World War II.
1944	National Congress of American Indians.

1945   World War II ends with the atomic bomb.
1947   Indian Claims Commission Act.
1948   Indians allowed to vote in Arizona.
1953   Liquor Prohibition repealed for Indians.
1954   Termination & Relocation Act.
1962   Indians allowed to vote in New Mexico.
1968   Indian Civil Rights Act.
1972   Indian Education Act.
1975   Indian Self-Determination & Education Assistance Act.
1978   American Indian Religious Freedom Act.
1978   Indian Child Welfare Act.
1988   Indian Gaming Regulatory Act.
1990   Indian Arts & Crafts Act.
1990   Native American Graves Protection & Repatriation Act
1992   Native American Languages Act.

"The only thing that I know for sure, is that I know nothing."
— Unknown

The 1887 Dawes Act, the 1934 Indian Reorganization Act, the 1954 Termination & Relocation Act, etc. were supposedly well-intentioned legislation to remedy past wrongs and help Native people toward prosperity and independence. However, when the dust settled at the end of each Act's tenure, the bottom line is that Native people have less than when they started.

It seems that Native people have been harmed as much by good intentions as by bad intentions. Although the bad intentions were more direct and brutal, the results are the same.

"The only thing that I know for sure, is that I know nothing."

—Unknown

There are very few absolutes in this life. The truth yesterday is not necessarily the truth today; and the truth today may not be the truth tomorrow. Truth is neither black or white but shades of gray, depending on the amount of knowledge at the time.

Truth can also be subjective, depending on your point of view. If you don't believe that truth is subjective, listen to lawyers or politicians present opposite views of the same issue. Or two witnesses to the same incident.

The truth is a blend of knowledge and perception. Truth and knowledge are strange companions because one often makes a liar of the other. Truth is like knowledge; the more you know, the more you realize there is to know.

The truth is generally a believable perception by someone that we consider a knowledgeable expert witness, even though those perceptions may be flawed by disinformation and/or misinformation.

Each person's truth is their perception of reality. When those perceptions are accepted as fact and are indelibly etched in the subconscious, it is very difficult to change people's minds. Especially, if those perceptions are to their advantage or in their best interest.

Where did Native People come from?

The prevalent theory is that, at least 12,000 years ago, Native American ancestors crossed the frozen Bering Straits, fanned out from Alaska and evolved into civilizations on two continents.

There is considerable speculation with regard to the origin and timeline of the arrival of the Native People to the continent. Theories are being studied that suggests Native People's history may be much older than has been generally accepted and they may be the descendants from multiple crossings of several different racial groups. Anthropology discovery based on new technology will substantiate or dismiss these theories.

Native People also have their own versions of origin and time.

Did Columbus discover America?

From the arrival of Columbus to the present, the truth about the Native People has been obscured by myth and misconception.

In 1492, Columbus accidentally landed in the Caribbean Islands while seeking a new trade route to the Far East.

We were taught in school that Christopher Columbus discovered America. The truth is that Columbus never set foot on the continent we know as America. Explorer Amerigo Vespucci was officially recognized for discovering and naming the Americas.

America was already discovered. Aztec, Mayan, Mound Builders, Pueblos and numerous other Native civilizations were comparable, and in some respects superior, to the contemporary civilizations in Europe.

Columbus was probably not even the first to explore the New World. An interesting book titled: "Columbus Was Last" by Patrick Hughey, offers the compelling premise that there were some 15–20 substantial foreign contacts prior to the arrival of Columbus.

Regardless of the circumstances, the arrival of Columbus to the New World was a historical accomplishment that initiated a chain of events that changed the world forever.

The "Indian" misnomer has been accepted to the extent that it is synonymous with all indigenous people in the western hemisphere.

Why were the Natives called "Indians?"

Columbus was convinced that he had landed in the East Indies, an India province, and called the native inhabitants "Indians." The "Indian" misnomer has been accepted to the extent that it is synonymous with all indigenous people in the western hemisphere.

"Manifest Destiny" & "Divine Providence"

Most Native Americans view the arrival of Columbus as the beginning of a 400-year cycle of diseases, exploitation, enslavement and genocide that devastated them as a race of people. We can only speculate about the massive number of Native people essentially exterminated by the attrition of genocide in 400 years. The ramifications of those sustained extermination policies exist today as shortened life expectancy due to emotional and health problems.

Settlers adopted doctrines of "manifest destiny" and "divine providence" as they moved steadily Westward.

After initial fears had subsided, most Native people were curious and even friendly toward the strange invaders. A touch of irony, some eastern tribes helped settlers survive the first critical winters. However, conflict between settlers and Native people was inevitable because their value system was simply not compatible with that of the settlers.

Many Native tribes had developed nomadic lifestyles that were in harmony with the seasons and environment. Their lifestyles were in direct conflict with the fixed homesteads, farms and industrial activity of the European settlers.

The concept of individual land ownership was alien to Native people. They believed the elements of the environment were inseparable and could not be owned by individuals. Their high regard for the environment was reflected by the inclusion of the elements in most religious ceremonies. The concept of Mother Earth and some special features of the land such as mountains are considered sacred. The issue was compounded by the idea that land ownership could be transferred by a piece of paper.

Settlers felt the Native people did not make good use of the land, therefore, they should yield to people who would use the land for more productive purposes. The settlers rationalized that Native people had no moral right to obstruct the expansion of a higher civilization. Settlers adopted doctrines of "manifest destiny" and "divine providence" as they moved steadily Westward.

For over 100 years, European nations made sporadic attempts to establish settlements along the Eastern seaboard. The first permanent settlement was Jamestown, an English colony established in 1607. The Pilgrims landed at Plymouth Rock in 1620. As other colonies were established, settlers began an aggressive policy of expansion by attrition.

Native tribes finally began to resist with open hostility. The first major retaliation occurred in 1622, when Powhatan leader

Opechancanough went on a rampage in Virginia and killed 347 settlers. The conflict initiated a pattern of reciprocal atrocities that lasted for nearly 300 years.

By the time the settlers were entrenched along the eastern seaboard, resentment and antagonism toward Native tribes had escalated. They were considered a sub-human race that must be removed or exterminated. The prevalent attitude tolerated and encouraged the practices of genocide and slavery.

During this same period of time, Spanish encroachment was taking place along the West coast and in the Southwest. Native people were brutalized and killed with impunity because they did not have a basis for legal recognition or recourse in the country. Native people could not bear witness against a white man in a court of law. Native people were not categorically granted citizenship until the Indian Citizenship Act in 1924.

During certain times, many colonies, states and territories paid bounties for Native people extermination. Bounties varied from $25 to $130 for each male scalp and usually half of that amount for women and children. "The only good Indian is a dead Indian" and "nits become lice" were typical expressions that reflected attitudes that lasted for 400 years.

The 1744 Treaty of Lancaster established the Appalachian Mountains as the physical boundary between the settlers and Native tribes. This general boundary was reaffirmed geographically when the 13 Colonies won their war for independence and became the United States of America.

As settlers' numbers multiplied, their insatiable demand for land forced Native tribes westward as they fought a losing battle for territory and survival. The conflicts became a war of bizarre perpetual retaliations. Historical records implicate both sides as participants in macabre atrocities.

However, most Native people fatalities were caused by diseases rather than by warfare. Native people had very little immunity

> *Bounties varied from $25 to $130 for each male scalp and usually half of that amount for women and children.*

By His EXCELLENCY

WILLIAM SHIRLEY, Efq;

Captain-General and Governor in Chief, in and over His Majesty's Province of the *Massachusetts-Bay*, in *New-England*, and Vice-Admiral of the fame, and Major-General in His Majesty's Army.

A PROCLAMATION.

 HEREAS the Indians of *Norridgewock, Arresagun'a-ook, Wewennock* and *St. John's* Tribes, and the Indians of the other Tribes inhabiting in the Eastern and Northern Parts of His Majesty's Territories of *New-England*, the *Penobscot* Tribe only excepted, have, contrary to their folemn Submiffion unto His Majesty long fince made and frequently renewed, been guilty of the most perfidious, barbarous and inhuman Murders of divers of his Majesty's *English* Subjects; and have abstained from all Commerce and Correspondence with His Majesty's faid Subjects for many Months past; and the faid *Indians* have fully discovered an inimical, traiterious and rebellious Intention and Disposition;

I have therefore thought fit to issue this Proclamation, and to Declare the Indians of the Norridgewock, Arresaguntacook, Wewennock and St. John's Tribes, and the Indians of the other Tribes new or late inhabiting in the Eastern and Northern Parts of His Majesty's Territories of New-England, and in Alliance and Confederacy with the above-recited Tribes, the Penobscots only excepted, to be Enemies, Rebels and Traitors to his Most Sacred Majesty: And I do hereby require His Majesty's Subjects of this Province to embrace all Opportunities of pursuing, captivating, killing and destroying all and any of the aforesaid Indians, the Penobscots excepted.

AND WHEREAS the General Court of this Province have voted, That a Bounty or Encouragement be granted and allowed to be paid out of the Publick-Treasury to the marching Army that fhall be employed for the Defence of the Eastern and Western Frontiers from the Twenty-fifth of this Month of *June* until the Twenty-fifth of *November* next;

I have thought fit to publish the fame; and I do hereby promise, That there fhall be paid out of the Province-Treasury to all and any of the said Forces, over and above their Bounty upon Enlistment, their Wages and Subsistence, the Premiums or Bounties following, viz.

For every Male Indian Prisoner above the Age of Twelve Years, that fhall be taken and brought to *Boston*, *Fifty Pounds*.

For every Male Indian Scalp, brought in as Evidence of their being killed, *Forty Pounds*.

For every Female Indian Prisoner, taken and brought in as aforesaid, and for every Male Indian Prisoner under the Age of Twelve Years, taken and brought in as aforesaid, *Twenty-five Pounds*.

For every Scalp of such Female Indian or Male Indian under Twelve Years of Age, brought as Evidence of their being killed, as aforesaid, *Twenty Pounds*.

GIVEN under my Hand at Boston, in the Province aforesaid, this Twelfth Day of June, 1755, and in the Twenty-eighth Year of the Reign of our Sovereign Lord GEORGE the Second, by the Grace of GOD, of Great-Britain, France, and Ireland, KING, Defender of the Faith, &c.

By His Excellency's Command,
J. WILLARD, Sec'y.

W. Shirley.

GOD Save the KING.

BOSTON: Printed by John Draper, Printer to His   the Honourable His Majesty's COUNCIL. 1755.

In 1755, the British crown offered 40 pounds for Indian male scalps and 20 pounds for females and children.

to European diseases that were introduced to them as a matter of course, but sometimes by design.

Smallpox, cholera, malaria, syphilis and influenza are a few of the diseases that decimated the Native population. Many tribes were essentially wiped out by the thousands. In some instances, the devastation was so complete that pious settlers considered the epidemics as "divine providence."

Survivors of disease and genocide were subject to the widespread practice of slavery. Native people were sold as slaves to work plantations and mines. Conquest has been standard operating procedure since man became "civilized"— even among Native people. The victims of conquest suffer "man's inhumanity to man." Native tribes practiced bondage and other atrocities as rituals of intertribal warfare for centuries. However, the white slave traders escalated the practice to the scale of commercial enterprise.

The 1830 Indian Removal Act, signed into law by President Andrew Jackson, extinguished Native tribal land rights east of the Mississippi. It provided for their relocation to "Indian Country," which was defined as "the part of the United States West of the Mississippi and not within the states of Missouri, Louisiana or the territory of Arkansas."

This definitive boundary seemed to create a brief pause in the settlers' voracious appetite for Native tribal lands. However, an ominous tidal wave of immigrants was building along the western frontier.

By 1850, the United States had extinguished all European land claims from coast to coast, setting the stage for the settlement of the West. Only the Native tribes stood in the way of progress.

The 1854 Indian Appropriation Act gave Congress the authority to establish Indian Reservations. The act provided the legal basis for removal of specific Native tribes to specific locations. In 1862, President Lincoln signed the Homestead Act and Railroad Act into law which became major factors in crushing Native tribal resistance.

Many tribes were essentially wiped out by the thousands. In some instances, the devastation was so complete that pious settlers considered the epidemics as "divine providence."

Equal integration seems to require a more resolute will from some racial groups than others.

The discovery of gold in the West and availability of free land launched a stampede of humanity across the land. When the dust settled, Native tribal land rights had essentially been extinguished and the devastated Native people had nearly been exterminated. In the wake of this carnage, the western half of a new nation was born.

> *"We the people of the United States, in order to form a more perfect Union, establish justice, insure domestic tranquility, provide for the common defense, promote the general welfare, and secure the blessings of liberty to ourselves and our posterity, do ordain and establish this Constitution for the United States of America."*
> — Preamble to the Constitution, 1776

A case in point: In the early 1800s, there were an estimated 260,000 Native people in California: by 1900, there were 20,000 survivors.

By 1890, the last of the Indian wars were over, and the 1887 Indian Dawes Allotment Act was the "coup de grace" for Native tribal land rights. The essence of this act was to eliminate the rights of Native people to hold tribal land in common. Those rights were exchanged for individualized allotments of 160 acres per head of household, with lesser acreages to individuals. The 1860 surplus land was ceded to the government and sold to the settlers. More than 100 reservations were allotted and over 90 million acres were abstracted from Indian lands.

In less than 100 years, Native tribal lands had been reduced from all land west of the Appalachian Mountains to desolate reservations totaling less than 4% of the continental United States.

During the development of America, tremendous hardships were endured by immigrants of all races. There has always been a "pecking order" as each new ethnic group struggled to overcome

continued on page 35

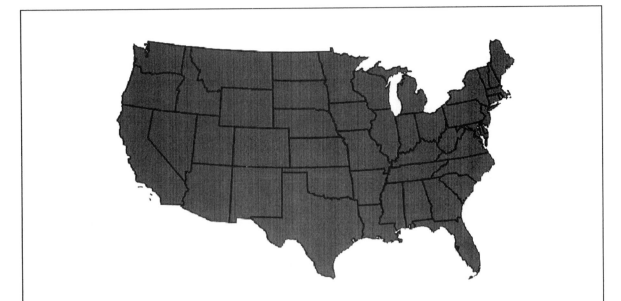

1492: Arrival of Columbus

There is considerable speculation with regard to the origin and timeline of the arrival of Native Americans to the continent. Technology is providing the means for scientific discovery that indicates that Native American history may be much older than has been generally accepted. Native Americans also have their own versions of origin and time.

The prevalent theory is that, at least 12,000 years ago, Native American ancestors crossed the frozen Bering Straits, fanned out from Alaska and evolved into civilizations on two continents.

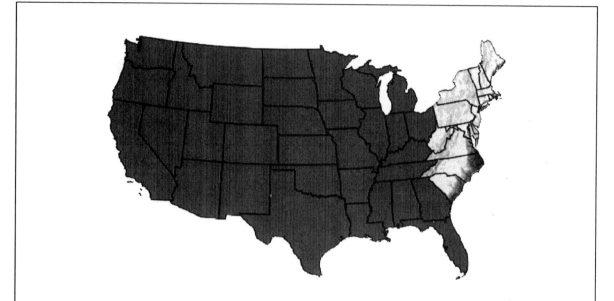

1790: Indians Forced Inland

For over 100 years, European nations made sporadic attempts to establish settlements along the Eastern seaboard. The first permanent settlement was Jamestown, and English colony established in 1607. The Pilgrims landed at Plymouth Rock in 1620. As other colonies were established, settlers began an aggressive policy of expansion by attrition.

Indians resisted with open hostility. The first major retaliation occurred in 1622, when Powhatan leader Opechancanough went on a rampage in Virginia and killed 347 settlers. The conflict initiated a pattern of reciprocal atrocities that lasted for nearly 300 years.

The 1744 Treaty of Lancaster established the Appalachian Mountains as the physical boundary between the settlers and Indians. this general boundary was reaffirmed geographically when the 13 Colonies won their war for independence and became the United States of America.

By 1671, there were 50,000 settlers in the Colonies.

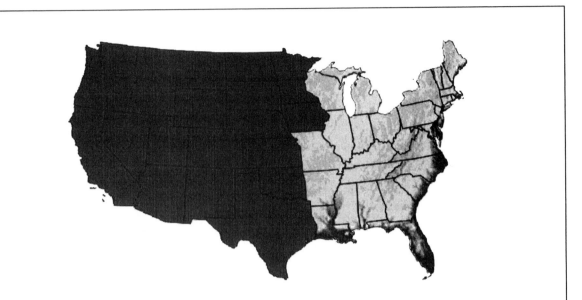

1830: Indian Country

The 1830 Indian Removal Act, signed into law by President Andrew Jackson, extinguished Indian land rights east of the Mississippi. It provided for their relocation to "Indian Country," which was defined as "the part of the United States West of the Mississippi and not within the states of Missouri, Louisiana or the territory of Arkansas."

This definitive boundary seemed to create a brief pause in the settlers' voracious appetite for Indian lands. However, an ominous tidal wave of immigrants was building along the western frontier.

By 1829, the population of the United States was 12.5 million.

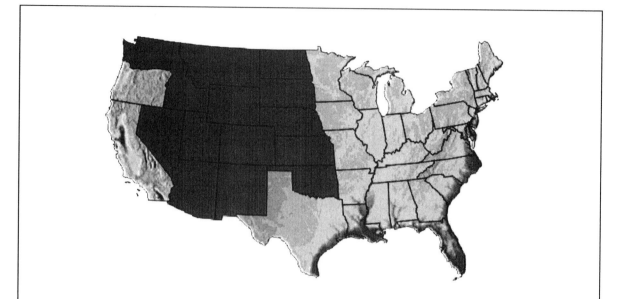

1860: Immigrant Stampede

By 1850, the United States had extinguished all European land claims from coast to coast, setting the stage for the settlement of the West. Only the Indians stood in the way of progress.

The 1854 Indian Appropriation Act gave Congress the authority to establish Indian Reservations. The act provided the legal basis for removal of specific Indians to specific locations. In 1862, President Lincoln signed the Homestead Act and Railroad Act into law that became major factors in crushing Indian resistance.

The discovery of gold in the West and availability of free land launched a stampede of humanity across the land. When the dust settled, Indian land rights had essentially been extinguished and the devastated Indian had nearly been exterminated. In the wake of this carnage, the western half of a new nation was born.

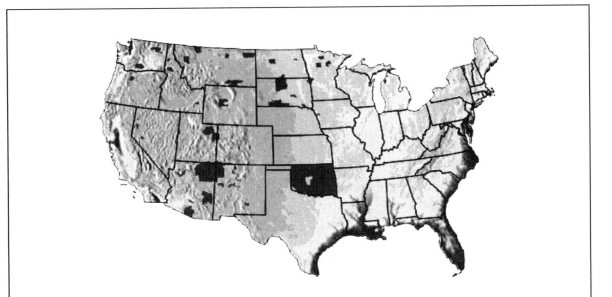

1890: The Vanquished Indian

By 1890, the last of the Indian wars was over, and the 1887 Indian Allotment Act was the "coup de grace" for Indian tribal land rights. The essence of this act was to eliminate the rights of Indians to hold tribal land in common. Those rights were exchanged for individualized allotments of 160 acres per head of household, with lesser acreages to individuals. The 1860 surplus land was ceded to the government and sold to the settlers. More than 100 reservations were allotted and over 90 million acres were abstracted from Indian lands.

In less than 100 years, Indian lands had been reduced from all land west of the Appalachian Mountains to desolate reservations totaling less than 4% of the continental United States.

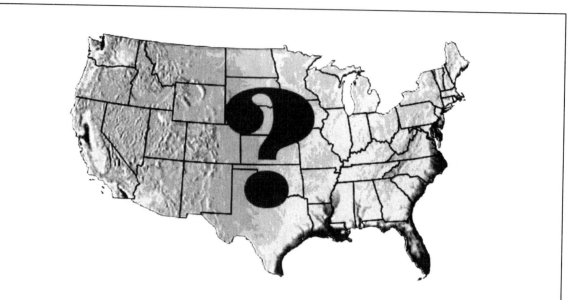

2100: Native American Lands?

"The utmost good faith shall always be through the legal system, observed toward the Indians; their land and property shall never be taken from them without their consent; and in their property, rights and liberty, they shall never be invaded or disturbed, unless in just and lawful wars authorized by Congress; but laws founded on justice and humanity shall from time to time be made, for preventing wrongs done to them, and for preserving peace and friendship with them."

— United States Congress Northwest Ordinance, 1787

continued from page 28
racial prejudice and weave their particular talents into the fabric of America. Equal integration seems to require a more resolute will from some racial groups than others.

Native tribes fought for their inalienable aboriginal land rights. The fierce resistance resulted in 400 years of Native people bashing that left a physically deteriorated people with deep psychological wounds. Native people had lost their land, self-image, self-esteem and were rapidly becoming a vanishing race.

Ironically, during intense oppression of the Native people, the United States fought the Revolutionary War for freedom and independence. The Emancipation Proclamation, President Lincoln's declaration to free the black race from slavery, was a cornerstone of the Civil War. These lofty ideals were to establish the moral fiber and political creed of the United States.

> *"We hold these truths to be self-evident, that all men are created equal, that they are endowed by their Creator with certain unalienable Rights, that among these are Life, Liberty and the pursuit of Happiness."*
> Declaration of Independence – 1776

The rhetorical question is, "Could the Native people dilemma have been resolved in a more humane and equitable manner?" Probably not, within the context of the times.

Groundless treaties

Because Native tribes were the sole inhabitants of the North American continent, it was imperative for European nations to establish a legal concept of aboriginal land rights as a basis for treaty negotiations. Treaties became the legal basis used by encroaching settlers to appropriate Native tribal lands.

Treaties became the legal basis used by encroaching settlers to appropriate Native tribal lands.

Treaties were interpreted to Native tribal leaders who rarely knew what was actually written on the document placed before them for mark or signature.

Typical treaty negotiations were based on huge Native tribal land cessions in exchange for reservation areas, food, hardware goods and annuity payments. During the translation from document to reality, questionable sincerity succumbed to avarice and self-serving rationalization. The government's "perpetual guaranty" of Native tribal lands did not endure; and the delivery of food, goods and monies failed to match the promises.

Native tribes were at a distinct disadvantage during treaty negotiations because the treaty documents were written in a language Native people did not understand. Treaties were interpreted to Native tribal leaders who rarely knew what was actually written on the document placed before them for mark or signature. Other ruses included negotiation of a treaty with a manageable Native who did not represent the tribe or plying the negotiators with whiskey.

Hundreds of treaties were negotiated between Native tribes and European settlers from early colonial days to the establishment of the United States. In 1778, the United States government entered into its first official treaty with the Delawares. At least 370 documented treaties were negotiated and ratified by Congress during the next 100 years.

In 1871, Congress declared that no Indian nation would be recognized for the purpose of making treaties. By then, Native tribes realized that treaty negotiations had become a charade of empty promises based on fraud and deceit for the convenience of the government and the benefit of the land-hungry settlers.

An inherent stipulation in these treaty negotiations was the trust responsibility of the United States government to provide for the health, education and entitlement of the Native people. The general consensus in the Native American community is that government has not lived up to its trust responsibilities. These issues have not been resolved to an equitable conclusion. Some Native tribes and organizations are seeking reparations through the legal system.

"The utmost good faith shall always observed toward the Indians; their land and property shall never be taken from them without their consent; and in their property, rights and liberty, they shall never be invaded or disturbed, unless in just and lawful wars authorized by Congress; but laws founded on justice and humanity shall from time to time be made, for preventing wrongs done to them, and for preserving peace and friendship with them."
— United States Congress Northwest Ordinance, 1787

Vanquished Native People

"Give me your tired, your poor your huddled masses yearning to breathe free, the wretched refuse of your teeming shore. Send these, the homeless, tempest tossed to me. I lift my lamp beside the golden door."
— Statue of Liberty Inscription, 1903

By 1890, the physically battered Native people were decimated. Those remaining were confined to desolate reservations with their daily regimen of hardships, humiliation and exploitation. The once fearsome warrior had been reduced to a despised beggar, thief and a nuisance. The reservation system served to keep Native people out of sight and under control. Native tribes essentially became wards of the government, whose needs were given a very low priority.

The vanquished Native tribes became a favorite subject of the media. Their plight was compounded by the invention of motion pictures. The nation's concept of Native people was the indelible celluloid images created by Hollywood westerns for entertainment. Marauding savage hordes became villainous anti-heroes as they attacked hopelessly outnumbered courageous settlers. Native people became a maligned blur of fact and fiction. The movie blitz was so effective that most fictitious perceptions still exist today.

> *Native people became a maligned blur of fact and fiction. The movie blitz was so effective that most fictitious perceptions still exist today.*

37

In the last few years, movies such as *Dances With Wolves, Black Robe, Thunderheart* and *Incident at Oglala,* were efforts to present a more realistic image and history of Native people.

Today, a new cadre of talented Native people in the entertainment industry are creating, organizing and producing their own version of Native people history and stories. Productions about Native people, can never have the innate authenticity of productions by Native people. Native people should tell Native people stories.

America's Holocaust

There have been numerous studies regarding the Native people population when Columbus reached the New World. Most studies included North and South America with estimates that ranged from 5 to 30 million

American Indian Holocaust and Survival – A Population History Since 1492, published in 1987 by Author Russell Thornton, is a very interesting definitive study of American Indian population before and after the arrival of Columbus. (Mr. Thornton's book is available in most libraries, bookstores and also Amazon.com)

The consensus is that, when the Europeans began to occupy the New World, there were 5 million Native people existing as some 500 tribes ranging in size from a few dozen to several thousand, speaking some 500 languages.

Mr. Thornton's hypothesis indicates that there were approximately 5 million Native people within the continental United States at the arrival of Columbus to the New World. Five million Native people divided by 500 tribes = 10,000 people average for each tribe. Even with the larger tribes scattered in bands and clans, those are awfully big tribes! Was there enough food supply to support these numbers?

Two disturbing hypothetical questions come to mind based on Mr. Thornton's research:

❖ Assuming there were 5 million Native people around 1500 and 237,000 survivors in 1900, how many millions of Native people were essentially exterminated over a 400-year period, either directly and indirectly, as a result of European contact?

❖ Secondly, if the 1492 Native population of 5 million had continued to increase at a normal rate, what would be the Native American population today?

The Jewish Holocaust of 6 million people is the only event that can begin to be used for comparison.

In 1890, the Census Bureau officially counted 248,000 American Indians for the first time. By 1900, there were 237,000 survivors.

"I am tired of fighting. Our chiefs are killed...It is cold and we have no blankets. The little children are freezing to death...Hear me, my chiefs, I am tired, my heart is sick and sad. From where the sun now stands I will fight no more forever."

— Nez Perce Chief Joseph, 1877

Notes:

_____

_____

_____

_____

_____

_____

_____

_____

_____

_____

_____

Native American tribes have a blood quantum dilemma. Theoretically, the blood quantum gene pool will become more diluted with each succeeding generation until it is extinguished. This is happening very rapidly to urban Native Americans, which constitutes 78% of the Native American population. Urban Native people are the largest tribe of all.

S e c t i o n   2 :

The Present

Native people mixed inter-tribally for thousands of years and inter-racially for the last 500 years. The result is many generations of mixed blood Native people.

Before we get into demographics and statistics, keep this caveat in mind:

"There are three kinds of lies: lies, damned lies and statistics."
— Mark Twain

Demographic data is utilized to make projections if a certain course of action is taken or continued. Hopefully, the conclusions will be a catalyst to initiate dialogue with regard to the long-term future of the Native American people.

POPULATION

Genetic roulette

Northwest tribes had distinct physical features that were different from the Southwest tribes; and the Plains tribes looked different than Eastern tribes. Today, there is usually a core population of each tribe that still has some of those physically distinct features of their respective tribes, but as mobility and inter-tribal marriages increased, the physical differences have become blurred.

Native people mixed inter-tribally for thousands of years and inter-racially for the last 500 years. The result is many generations of mixed blood Native people. Native tribes often integrated by arrangement, to preclude genetic contamination of a limited gene pool (cousins marrying cousins). As a result, most Native Americans are tribally hyphenated (Pima-Maricopa-Navajo-Hopi, etc).

A large segment of today's Native Americans are also racially hyphenated (Navajo-Pima-Apache-English-Hispanic-Irish, etc). These two genetic realities raise some thorny issues. Who is and who isn't considered to be Native American, either by legal definition or by self-identification, has become an important issue for Native Americans and their respective tribes. Contrary to the stereotypical image, today's Native Americans come in all sizes, shapes and colors. At any major Pow Wow, conference or trade show, the color spectrum will range from blue-eyed blonds to the African features of the "buffalo soldiers" and everything in between.

Who is legally considered Native American?

The United States government definition of a "legal" Indian:

Any person who has the certifiable Indian blood quantum to meet the enrollment requirements of a federally recognized tribe.

This seemingly innocuous definition has been the cause of enormous dilemma in the Native American communities. Each tribe has the right to determine the minimum blood quantum requirements for enrollment. Most tribes require 1/4 minimum blood quantum for enrollment. Native Americans are the only race of people who must legally prove that they are Native American. (Other races are accepted at face value. No pun intended.)

At one end of the spectrum: the Cherokee Nation of Oklahoma is known for the most liberal enrollment. They accept anyone who can trace their linear ancestry to the Dawes Commission of Final Rolls compiled between the years of 1899–1906, regardless of blood quantum. Some enrolled Cherokees have a minute trace of Native American blood such as 1/512 or less. This liberal policy has increased Cherokee Nation enrollment to well over 300,000. Other Cherokee Tribes have more stringent enrollment requirements.

Joke: Some Cherokees have to be careful shaving because if they cut themselves, they may lose all of their Indian blood.

At the other end of the spectrum: the Northern Utes of Utah require 5/8 minimum blood quantum for membership.

"It affords me sincere pleasure to be able to apprise you of the entire removal of the Cherokee Nation of Indians to their new homes West of the Mississippi ... their removal has been principally under the conduct of their own chiefs, and they have migrated without any apparent reluctance."
— President Martin Van Buren, 1838

What is the US Native American population?

Census 2000 estimates:

There are approximately 2.4 million self-identified Native Americans in the United States. Self-identified means there is a box on the Census 2000 form that says Native American — if you mark the box, you are counted as Native American. (Census 2000 also asks for tribal affiliation which should be very interesting.)

Of that 2.4 million, approximately 1.4 million are tribally enrolled. (This indicates that approximately 1 million people consider themselves Native American but are not enrolled.)

Anthropologists estimate there are some 15 million people who have a discernible degree of Native American blood, but have lost their tribal connection. (Recent mitochondrial DNA studies suggests that the number may be much larger than 15 million.)

The 1990 Census counted 1,959,234 Native Americans. Native Americans were undercounted by some 12% making them the most undercounted minority in the country. The undercount cost Native American communities countless millions of dollars in federal services and programs.

Census 2000 is in the final stages of enumeration and compilation. Census 2000 is making the effort to do a much better job of counting Native Americans than in 1990. Partnerships were developed with the Urban and Reservation communities by hiring Native people as administrators and enumerators to count Native people. We await the final count with great anticipation. The Native American Online portal will be linked to the statistics.

Tribal "full bloods"?

The term "full-blood" is the designation for Native Americans who consider themselves to have 100% blood quantum of one tribe. Is this possible or does "full-blood" at best mean composite tribal Native People blood? The designation seems to be more of a reference to tribal spirituality and tradition than definitive tribal blood quantum.

Tribally "mixed bloods"?

Inter-tribal and clan mixing was a natural process to preclude genetic inbreeding. It was accepted custom to seek a mate from a neighboring tribe or clan. The creation of the reservation system and forced relocation of tribes accelerated the inter-tribal melting pot.

Oklahoma Native Tribal Relocation

The most notorious example was the relocation of some 60 tribes from all parts of the country to Oklahoma territory during the 1800s.

The large concentration of tribes relocated to Oklahoma came from a wide range of geographic areas. Consequently, Oklahoma Native American history presents a much larger view of Native America than is indicated by the relatively small geographic area.

> *"It affords me sincere pleasure to be able to apprise you of the entire removal of the Cherokee Nation of Indians to their new homes West of the Mississippi...their removal has been principally under the conduct of their own chiefs, and they have migrated without any apparent reluctance."*
> — President Martin Van Buren, 1838

Who are "racially mixed-bloods"?

Settler, pioneer and frontier life in early America was a perilous regimen of hardships. Consequently, there was an acute shortage of European women. Because of the imbalance, sexual interaction between European men and Native women was an inevitable and common practice.

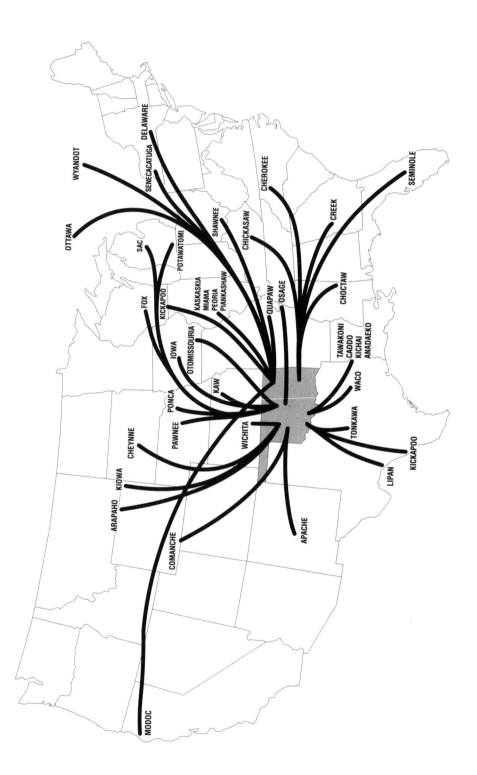

On the basis of this premise, there is the strong probability that there is Native people blood in the veins of a much larger segment of the population than was recorded or acknowledged. Since World War II, there is more of an inclination to acknowledge a Native skeleton in the family closet.

The premise of racial blood mixing can be compared to the black slavery experience and the proliferation of mixed blood children as an aftermath of military occupation in foreign lands. Consensual and non-consensual sexual activity has always been considered a military prerogative during territorial conquest and occupation. "The brotherhood of man" may be a much more appropriate expression than we realize.

Since World War II, there is more of an inclination to acknowledge a Native skeleton in the family closet.

Hyphenated Native People?

Theoretically, if a Navajo man marries a Hopi woman, and their Navajo-Hopi son marries a Sioux-Crow girl; and if their Navajo-Hopi-Sioux-Crow son marries a Pima-Supai-Apache-Ute girl; their grandchildren are Navajo-Hopi-Sioux-Crow-Pima-Supai-Apache-Ute.

Some tribes are beginning to see the "handwriting on the wall." The Cherokee Nation of Oklahoma and recently, the Crow Tribe of Montana have modified their blood quantum requirements to linear descendancy. Some tribes have modified their enrollment criteria to accept other composite tribal blood. Tribes do not allow membership in more than one tribe.

There are Native American families who have lived in Native American communities, sometimes for generations, who do not have official records to document blood quantum required for enrollment certification.

Most Native tribes did not have written languages. During periods of relocation and assimilation, genealogy often became a matter of oral interpretation. Most Native American languages were difficult for Europeans to understand and pronounce, so when the enumerator couldn't pronounce the 8 syllable Native name, the person became John Jackson, Joe Smith, etc. A combination of oral and sign language became the basis for communication. As a result, Native Americans were often given arbitrary anglicized names for the records.

During World War I and World War II, the Native Americans volunteered and distinguished themselves in disproportionately large numbers. Having Native American blood became socially acceptable. Since Native American casinos have begun to prosper, the interest in establishing a Native American connection has increased dramatically. It seems that everyone who has a remote Native American relative wants to be recognized as a Native American and enrolled if possible.

Where do Native Americans live?

In 1990, the Navajo reservation had 143,405 people; Pine Ridge was second with 11,182 and eight reservations had between 7,000 to 10,000 people. Most reservations had less than 1,000 people. About half of all Native people live on the 10 largest reservations.

Who are Urban Native Americans?

One of the major issues for Urban Native Americans is tribal members who do not reside on their reservations have limited relations with the BIA and IHS, since BIA and IHS programs are primarily administered for members who live on or near reservations. And yet off-reservation members are included in the count as a basis for program allocations.

From the turn of the century until World War 11, Native Americans were subjected to the coercion of boarding schools, assimilation and relocation programs. The idea of this period of cultural genocide was to "kill the Indian and save the child."

During World War II, 25,000 Native Americans left the reservations to serve in the armed forces. After the war, migrations accelerated to seek employment, education and opportunity.

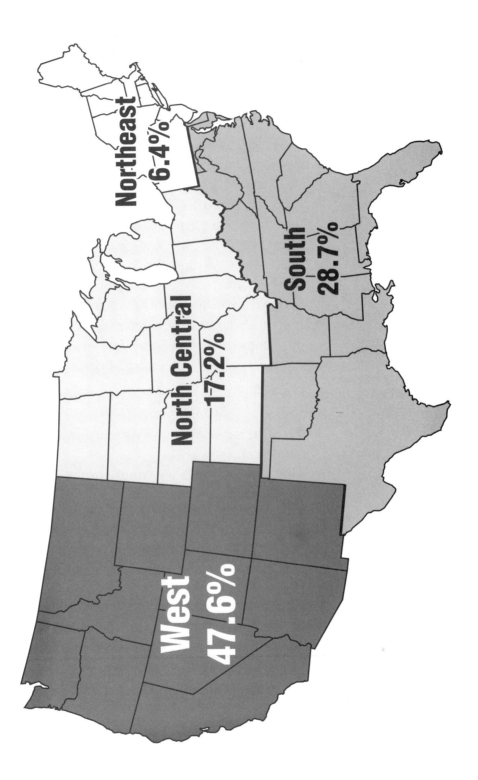

Composition of today's urban Native American community:

❖ Enrolled members who live and work off-reservation, but are still closely connected by family and sometimes have a reservation residence.

❖ Geographically relocated enrolled "at large" members by lineal descent or affiliated by marriage.

❖ People who have a Native American ancestor and are not enrolled, but are active in the community and consider themselves Native Americans traditionally and spiritually.

❖ People who have an Native American ancestor — generations removed, who have lost their tribal connection and are not active in the Native American in community.

❖ Most reservation Native Americans and urban Native Americans have close family ties and interact culturally. Many urban Native Americans live near their respective reservations.

According to 1990 Census there were:

❖ 437,431 reservation Native Americans. (22% of the total population.)

❖ 1,436,105 urban Native Americans. (78% of the total population.)

Native American population is further complicated by the evolution of two categories: Reservation Native Americans and Urban Native Americans. For the most part, this division of Native Americans is a circumstance of birth.

Native Americans who are born and become adults on the reservation will generally stay on or near the reservation or return if they should leave. For Native Americans born off-reservation, the chances of returning are remote, especially if the family migration happened generations ago and if they relocated geographically.

Are Native tribes programmed for extinction?

This situation creates an internal dilemma: Reservation Native Americans receive the direct benefits of federal programs such as housing, utility subsidies, health care, education and economic development aid, while their enrolled urban counterparts are essentially excluded from most of these programs. Even though the enrolled Urban Native Americans are included in the head count as a basis for procurement from these programs.

Our campaign to get population and enrollment numbers directly from the tribes met with lukewarm response (about 25%). An important feature of the Native American Online portal is the network of tribal websites where the tribes can control and post their own information.

There are 3 critical issues facing Native America with regard to the population and continuity of future generations:

❖ The dilution of blood-quantum.

❖ Nurture Urban Native people connections.

❖ Loss of tribal language.

Blood quantum is the cause of considerable division and inequities in the Native American community. An example: some Oklahoma Cherokees have a minute trace (such as 1/512) of Native blood and are enrolled tribal members, while other tribally mixed-bloods have considerable composite blood but are not enrolled because they do not have the specific blood quantum to meet any of their respective tribal requirements.

There is no solution that will satisfy or include everyone. The cold hard facts of life is that some people are going to be excluded who should be included; and some people will be included who should be excluded. Do the issues have black and white answers, or does the solution lie in the gray area of compromise?

It is not appropriate, prudent or moral that the children and grandchildren of tribal members are not members of the same tribe

It is not appropriate, prudent or moral that the children and grandchildren of tribal members are not members of the same tribe as their grandfathers.

> *In affairs of the heart, 21 year-old hormones do not have much regard for blood quantum or tribal affiliation.*

as their grandfathers. The bottom line is that theoretically, the Native American gene pool will become smaller with each generation until it is extinguished. This is happening very rapidly to urban Native Americans, which constitutes 78% of the Native American population. Urban Native people are the largest tribe of all.

22% of the Native American population live on reservations — which means that 78% live in the cities. Seven out of 10 Native Americans do not marry other Native Americans. Do the math and project those numbers a couple of generations. The 78% will be disconnected and the 22% will be severely diminished unless some dramatic changes are made.

The question has been asked: Why don't Native Americans marry other Native Americans? In affairs of the heart, 21 year-old hormones do not have much regard for blood quantum or tribal affiliation.

In order to survive politically and genetically, Native tribes must develop an inclusive rather than exclusive philosophy and agenda. Acknowledgment doesn't necessary mean enrollment, it could mean affiliation.

When Tribal people argue internally about who is and who isn't a tribal member, they are unwittingly, participating in the US Government strategy of "divide and conquer." Whether by design or attrition, identity politics is an invention of the US government and its still working very well today! It is foolish to criticize one another for cultural and racial dilution that was initiated by the US government. In this sense, we have become our own worst enemy

Native people struggle with the enrollment process to become members of their own tribes, yet they are citizens of the United States simply be being born.

The pendulum has swung from being inclusive (when the ranks were limited by the US government) to being exclusive because there are resources and benefits. And lets be honest, it's mostly based on greed! Greed is not necessarily a bad thing but it cannot become more important than the continuity of future generations.

Wiser souls must look at the bigger picture, because immediate benefits are not worth the long-term loss of people. It's ironic that the Native people who would not yield to the yoke; those who hid in the hills and were never enrolled, are the ones excluded.

It is human nature, but arrogant, for people to take credit for their birth circumstances. If you are born with blond hair and blue eyes, you had nothing to do with it. Or if you were lucky enough to be born Native American, or born on the reservation, you had absolutely nothing to do with it. Blood quantum is not a matter of choice. It's the luck of the draw.

We are the lucky ones, the ones that by circumstances, not by choice, that still have that precious tribal connection, why would we not be generous and kind by embracing our less fortunate relatives?

Reservation Native Americans and their Urban relatives need each other.

> *In April 2000, William Mehojah the last full-blooded member of the Kaw tribe, died at 82.*

Ishi, the last Yahi Yana

Some 200 tribes have become extinct. In 1911, a scraggly, raggedy Indian was discovered in Oroville, California foraging for food. He had existed in the mountains for years as the sole survivor of the Yahi Yana tribe that still had approximately 2,000 members in 1848. They named him Ishi which meant "man" in the Yana language. He died in 1916.

The last Kaw "full-blood"

The Kaw, formerly known as the mighty Kansa tribe, controlled some 20 million acres that stretched across Northern Kansas into Nebraska and Missouri. In April 2000, William Mehojah the last full-blooded member of the Kaw tribe, died at 82. (Five years ago, there were 4 full-bloods.) Today, approximately 600 of 2439 enrolled members live on a 135 acre reservation in Oklahoma and most tribal members have only a fraction of Kaw blood.

Think of what a Native America looked like 100 years ago; and then try to imagine what a Native America will look like 100 years from today

How many Native languages still exist?

In 1492, approximately 500 Native languages were spoken in North America. Some were linked by "linguistic stocks" which meant that widely scattered tribal groups had some similarities in their languages.

Most of the 500 original languages of the Native tribes are already extinct. By 1995, 350 languages have become extinct. The remaining 150 are on the endangered list. Linguists predict that by 2020, 90 more languages will be extinct; and by 2050, only 20 Native American languages will still be spoken.

The language is the bedrock of any Native tribe's culture, traditions and spirituality. The languages are dying out with the Elders. Some parents are bilingual but their children and grandchildren are not much interested in learning their native language for a variety of reasons.

In 1990, Congress passed the Native American Languages Act but essentially provided no funding.

Mitochondrial DNA impact?

In 10 or 20 years, a DNA analysis should be available for say, $28. I believe that most people, including Native Americans, would be very surprised by the results. When you consider the fact that Americans have been mixing it up for 500 years and Native Americans for thousands of years. Who can say unequivocally, that they are 100% of anything?

This DNA scenario could be used against the Native Americans, if their claims are based on their tribal affiliation and some members may not meet the tribe's blood quantum requirements in the strictest sense.

The tribes use member numbers to get program money, but the services are not extended to the Native Americans once they leave the reservations. The scarcity of funds pits tribes against their urban counterparts.

Think of what a Native America looked like 100 years ago; and then try to imagine what a Native America will look like 100 years from today. The face of Native Americans looked quite different 100 years ago than it does today, and it will look quite different 100 years from today.

On a humanitarian basis, no one has the right to deny a person the acknowledgement of their ancestral origins.

TRIBES

What constitutes a Native tribe?

Originally, an Indian Tribe was a body of people bound together by blood ties who were socially, politically, and religiously organized, who lived together in a defined territory and who spoke a common language or dialect.

Native tribes formed as part of a natural process that evolved over thousands of years. Native tribal lifestyles and the limitations of the environment determined the number of people that could live in a given area. Native tribes social and political differences were important factors in the development of splinter clans, bands and tribes.

Each tribal history is a unique chapter in Native American History 101. Social scientists offer the premise that there may be other migration theories. For the purpose of our discussion, we will assume the prevalent theory that the Native tribal pyramid began as hunters crossed the Bering Straits in Alaska and began their migration over two continents.

The composition of today's tribes has been tremendously impacted by the Federal government's relocation programs and the reservation system. Multiple tribes were relocated on common reservations and some tribes were split and relocated to several different reservations.

> *The composition of today's tribes has been tremendously impacted by the Federal government's relocation programs and the reservation system.*

How many recognized tribes are there?

The United States government's legal definition for Indian tribes:

> *Any Indian tribe, band, nation, rancheria, pueblo, colony or community which is recognized by the United States government as eligible for programs and services provided by the Secretary of the Interior to Indians because of their status as Indians.*

❖ There are 559 Federally-recognized tribes in the US.

❖ There are 224 of those tribes are in Alaska.

❖ The spectrum ranges from several California tribal bands that have 2–3 members to the Cherokees of Oklahoma at over 350,000.

❖ Approximately 200 tribes are extinct.

❖ The 1954 Termination & Relocation Act terminated 61 tribes.

❖ 221 tribes are in various stages of petition for federal recognition. (These tribes range in size from small bands to the Lumbees of North Carolina with over 40,000 members.)

❖ Approximately 40 tribes are state-recognized.

What are petitioning tribes?

Petitioning for Federal recognition is a long, expensive and ambiguous process. Most tribes do not have the resources to sustain a petitioning process that requires indeterminate years of tenacious perseverance.

There are 7 basic requirements for Federal tribal recognition:

1. Historical documentation of Indian ancestry.
2. Proof of political influence over members.
3. A list of all tribal members.
4. Proof that members do not belong to another tribe.
4. A copy of the tribal governing document.

6. The presence of a distinct tribal community
7. The tribe must not be barred from a legal relationship with the US government.

Since 1978, 221 groups have submitted their petition for acknowledgment through the administrative process.

❖ Approximately 72 have submitted completed petitions.
❖ To date, 41 of these completed petitioners have been finally resolved.
❖ The current work load consists of 15 under active consideration.
❖ 11 ready for active consideration.
❖ Two decisions are in litigation.
❖ Four are in post-final decision appeal process before the Interior Board of Indian Appeals.

Each year, one or two tribes manage to navigate the arduous process and receive recognition. The Lumbees of North Carolina have been petitioning for over 100 years. The Little Shell Tribe of Chippewas of Montana were finally recognized in May, 2000 after petitioning for 108 years.

What is tribal sovereignty?

Each Native American tribe considers itself a sovereign nation. Many tribes have recently decided that the politically correct reference will be "nations" rather than tribes. The issue of sovereignty has been a subject of long-running debate between the United States government and the tribes. The United States government negotiated treaties with the tribes as sovereign nations and promised certain inalienable rights and entitlements in exchange for land cessions.

By definition, sovereignty is supreme and complete political independence and self-government. A sovereign nation must have the ability to defend its borders, exercise authority over its citizens, and conduct its business free from outside interference.

The United States government negotiated treaties with the tribes as sovereign nations and promised certain inalienable rights and entitlements in exchange for land cessions.

> *With the fervor of media attention focused on Indian gaming and the potential wealth it presents, many interest groups have formed and are embarking on new tactics to promote an anti-Indian sentiment.*

Tribal sovereignty is a paradox because the United States government, while recognizing the tribes as domestic sovereign nations, has perpetuated a relationship of tribal dependence on the government.

Does Potter Valley Rancheria in California at three acres and one Native American have the same sovereignty as the Navajo Nation with 17 million acres and 220,000 people? The smaller tribes need to find refuge under the protective umbrella created by the larger stronger tribes

The Interior Department has recently caused concern in the Native American community by its definition of "historic" tribes as those that have existed since time immemorial, whose powers derive from their unextinguished, inherent sovereignty.

"Non-historic" tribes are those created under the 1934 Indian Reorganization Act that have only powers incidental to owning property and conducting business. Another division.

Yesterday's promise — today's challenge

The following is an excerpt from the American Indian Research & Policy Institute – 1998

> Challenges to the legal tenets of tribal sovereignty are not entirely new, but they are of increasing intensity. With the fervor of media attention focused on Indian gaming and the potential wealth it presents, many interest groups have formed and are embarking on new tactics to promote an anti-Indian sentiment. Perceptions by these interest groups about Indian policy, such as hunting and fishing rights negotiated in treaties, are misconstrued into statements of "rights" granted to a "special" population (Indians) that are not afforded to all citizens. These misperceptions about the true legal and political status of American Indians fuel the fire to use the courts as a problem solver.

In addition, there is increased interaction between tribes and state governments that has a similar "chipping away" effect on the trust relationship between tribes and the U.S. Congress. This increased interaction follows years of disinterest on the part of state and local governments about the tribal people living on reservations; a disinterest that extended to American Indians living in urban areas as well. An example of the intensified relationships between tribal governments and state and local governments is the recent emphasis on taxing tribal governments for roads leading to and within Indian reservations or for funding other recreational activities, such as sports stadiums.

The federal government is reducing or attempting to eliminate its trust relationship with American Indian tribes through the devolution of social and economic support guaranteed to tribes. For example, the most recent welfare reform policies will cause tribes to deal with the state governments to access and acquire welfare benefits and other forms of social services for tribal members that were once funded under authority of the federal government. This pressure to forge relationships between tribes and state governments has the potential to critically alter the historical, legal, and sovereign relationship between tribes and the federal government both presently and in the future.

Challenges facing tribal governments from both internal and external forces remain a constant struggle for Indian leaders. In many ways, these challenges have changed little over time. Struggles over how tribes should be governed and by whom have been present since the inception of the Indian Reorganization Act of 1934. External pressures to reduce reservation land or to forfeit hunt-

> *The federal government is reducing or attempting to eliminate its trust relationship with American Indian tribes through the devolution of social and economic support guaranteed to tribes.*

These attacks on tribes and tribal sovereignty are propelled forward and are becoming increasingly more subtle.

ing and fishing rights have been a constant threat from state and local governments and non-Indian citizens.

These attacks on tribes and tribal sovereignty are propelled forward and are becoming increasingly more subtle. These threats seem to rely on the changing nature of internal tribal relations and tribal members' relationships to their reservations. Tribal leaders must return to or continue to utilize the strong foundation of traditional ways for governing their tribes. At the same time, tribal leaders and tribal members must possess an understanding of these current challenges, driven both internally and externally, and how these actions pose a tremendous threat to tribal sovereignty and American Indian tribes of the future.

How did tribes get their names?

Generally speaking, today's tribal names are the result of mangled pronunciations or hybrid designations by early trappers and settlers. Several tribes have recently changed their official names to reflect tribal languages: the Papago to Tohono O'Odham, Winnebago to Ho Chunk, Devil's Lake Sioux to Spirit Lake Nation, etc.

Jack D. Forbes, a professor at the University of California in Davis, California, published the *Atlas of Native History.* An interesting feature of the study is a list of tribal names in their respective Native American language referenced to the English version of the same name.

How do tribes govern themselves?

Most tribal governments are organized democratically, that is, with an elected leadership. The governing body is generally referred to as a "council" and comprised of persons elected by vote of the eligible adult tribal members. The presiding official is the "chairman," although some tribes use other titles such as "principal chief," "president" or "governor." An elected tribal council, recognized as such by the Secretary of the Interior, has authority to speak and act for the tribe and to represent it in negotiations with Federal State, and local governments.

Tribal governments generally define conditions of membership, regulate domestic relations of members, prescribe rules of inheritance for reservation property not in trust status, levy taxes, regulate property under tribal jurisdiction, control conduct of members by tribal ordinances, and administer justice.

Many tribes are organized under the Indian Reorganization Act (IRA) of 1934, including a number of Alaska Native villages, which adopted formal governing documents (Constitutions) under the provisions of a 1936 amendment to the IRA. The passage in 1971 of the Alaska Native Claims Settlement Act, however, provided for the creation of village and regional corporations under State law to manage the money and lands granted by the Act.

The Oklahoma Indian Welfare Act of 1936 provided for the organization of Indian tribes within the State of Oklahoma. Some tribes do not operate under any of these acts, but are nevertheless organized under documents approved of governments. Prior to reorganization, the tribes maintained their own, often highly developed, systems of self- government.

RESERVATIONS

How Many Reservations are there?

The United States government's legal definition of an Indian Reservation:

A Indian reservation is an area of land held in trust by the federal government, reserved for Indian use.

The Secretary of the Interior is the trustee for the United States. The Bureau of Indian Affairs (BIA) is responsible to the trustee for administration and management of Indian trust lands.

❖ There are 314 Federally recognized reservations, totaling some 55 million acres.

The 1830 Removal Act precipitated the infamous "Trail of Tears" that refers to the 1838 forced march of some 15,000 Cherokees from their coveted farmlands in the Southeastern United States to Oklahoma Native American territory. More than 4,000 Native Americans died during the march from disease, exposure and starvation.

— Approximately 44 million acres are tribal trust lands.

— Approximately 11 million acres are allotted lands.

❖ There are approximately 40 State-recognized reservations.

Native American reservations range in size from the one-acre Sheep Ranch Rancheria in California to the Navajo Nation at more than 17 million acres. A few reservations are nearly 100% tribal trust lands and others are almost entirely privately owned lands.

Do all tribes have reservations?

There are 559 Federally-recognized Tribes and 314 Federally-recognized reservations. Obviously, a significant number of Federally-recognized tribes do not have Federally-recognized reservations. There are 224 Federally-recognized tribes in Alaska and 37 in Oklahoma. There is one Federally-recognized reservation in Alaska (Annette Island) and one in Oklahoma (Osage).

What Resources are on Reservations?

It is poetic justice that some of the once-desolate reservations have become valuable land due to minerals resources, pristine resources and urban locations.

Some Native American tribes have an impressive array of resources on their reservation trust lands.

❖ 40% of United States uranium deposits.

❖ 30% of western coal reserves.

❖ 4% of United States oil and gas reserves.

❖ 44 million acres in range and grazing.

❖ 5.3 million acres of commercial forest.

❖ 2.5 million acres of crop area.

Historically, Native Americans are allowed to occupy lands until there is a greater need for the "common good" usually based on economic avarice. The acquisition is mandated by the Congressional political process. The cultivated lands of the five "civilized tribes" in the Southeastern states, discovery of gold in the Black Hills of South Dakota, and the discovery of oil in Oklahoma are just some explicit examples.

More recently, the budget cuts and control of Native American gaming issues are examples of control and manipulation by Congressional politics. The 120-year history of negotiations between Native Tribes versus the US government speaks for itself. Congress giveth and Congress can taketh away!

The 1830 Removal Act precipitated the infamous "Trail of Tears" that refers to the 1838 forced march of some 15,000 Cherokees from their coveted farmlands in the Southeastern United States to Oklahoma Native American territory. More than 4,000 Native Americans died during the march from disease, exposure and starvation.

In a broader context, the "Trail of Tears" was typical of the forced removal of some 60,000 members of the five "Civilized Tribes" (Cherokee, Creek, Chickasaw, Choctaw and Seminole) that lasted for nearly 10 years.

The forced removal was in violation of a Supreme Court decision by Chief Justice John Marshall in favor of the Native Americans, and President Andrew Jackson's infamous response: "John Marshall has made his decision, now let him enforce it."

The 120-year history of negotiations between Native Tribes versus the US government speaks for itself. Congress giveth and Congress can taketh away!

The Dawes Allottment Act

On February 8, 1887, Congress enacted the General Allotment Act (GAA). This Act directed the division of tribal lands and "allotment" of them to individual Indians. The purpose was to accelerate the "civilization" of Indians by making them private landowners, successful farmers, and ultimately to assimilate them into society at large. By the 1930's it was widely accepted that GAA had, for the most part, failed.

Congressman Henry Dawes, author of the act, once expressed his faith in the civilizing power of private property with the claim that to be civilized was to "wear civilized clothes...cultivate the ground, live in houses, ride in Studebaker wagons, send children to school, drink whiskey and own property."

An act to provide for the allotment of lands in severalty to Indians on the various reservations, and to extend the protection of the laws of the United States and the Territories over the Indians, and for other purposes.

Be it enacted, That in all cases where any tribe or band of Indians has been, or shall hereafter be, located upon any reservation created for their use, either by treaty stipulation or by virtue of an act of Congress or executive order setting apart the same for their use, the President of the United States be, and he hereby is, authorized, whenever in his opinion any reservation or any part thereof of such Indians is advantageous for agricultural and grazing purposes to cause said reservation, or any part thereof, to be surveyed, or resurveyed if necessary, and to allot the lands in said reservations in severalty to any Indian located thereon in quantities as follows:

To each head of a family, one-quarter of a section;

To each single person over eighteen years of age, one-eighth of a section;

To each orphan child under eighteen years of age, one-eighth of a section; and,

To each other single person under eighteen years now living, or who may be born prior to the date of the order of the President directing an allotment of the lands embraced in any reservation, one-sixteenth of a section;
...

SEC. 5. That upon the approval of the allotments provided for in this act by the Secretary of the Interior, he shall ... declare that the United States does and will hold the land thus allotted, for the period of twenty-five years, in trust for the sole use and benefit of the Indian to whom such allotment shall have been made, ... and that at the expiration of said period the United States will convey the same by patent to said Indian, or his heirs as aforesaid, in fee, discharged of such trust and free of all charge or encumbrance whatsoever: ...

SEC. 6. That upon the completion of said allotments and the patenting of the lands to said allottees, each and every member of the respective bands or tribes of Indians to whom allotments have been made shall have the benefit of and be subject to the laws, both civil and criminal, of the State or Territory in which they may reside; ... And every Indian born within the territorial limits of the United States to whom allotments shall have been made under the provisions of this act, or under any law or treaty, and every Indian born within the territorial limits of the United States who has voluntarily taken up, within said limits, his residence separate and apart from any tribe of Indians therein, and has adopted the habits of civilized life, is hereby declared to be a citizen of the United States, and is entitled to all the rights, privileges, and immunities of such citizens, whether said Indian has been or not, by birth or otherwise, a member of any tribe of Native Americans within the territorial limits of the United States without in any manner impairing or otherwise affecting the right of any such Indian to tribal or other property.

Impact Of Allotment

What is mixed or checkerboard land ownership and how did it happen? Mixed land ownership describes the pattern of land ownership often resembling a checkerboard that exists on many reservations. Title to the land is held by different entities including the tribe, Native American individuals, the state,

Why are these treaty lands now owned by non-Indian entities, creating mixed land ownership on many reservations?

the county, the federal government and non-Indian groups or individuals.

When tribes signed treaties they gave up millions of acres of aboriginal territory for designated reservation areas. Why are these treaty lands now owned by non-Indian entities, creating mixed land ownership on many reservations? For most tribes, mixed land ownership began with the Dawes Act better known as the Allotment Act passed in 1887. Prior to the passage of this Act all lands within the boundaries of the reservation were owned by tribes as stipulated in their respective treaties or executive orders.

Outside interests, such as timber, railroad companies, and homesteaders, wanted more Native American land and sought to gain use and control of select lands within reservation treaty boundaries. These entities put pressure on the federal government to allow access and title to these lands.

In total disregard of the treaties, the Dawes Act was implemented. Individual tribal members were allotted 160, 80, and 40-acre parcels. Remaining reservation (treaty) lands were declared surplus and sold to non-Indians through surplus land sales.

The Allotment Act was one of the most devastating pieces of legislation ever passed in terms of reduction of tribally owned lands, breakdown of Native tribal culture, and creation of some of the greatest bureaucratic barriers to Indians use and control of the land base. This action was in direct violation of the treaty agreements. Prior to the Allotment Act tribal land holdings totaled 138 million acres. By the end of the allotment period in 1934, nearly 90 million acres held passed out of Native tribal ownership.

The Indian Land Working Group

In 1991, the 1st Annual Indian Land Consolidation Symposium was held in Pendleton, Oregon and was co-sponsored by the Confederated Tribes of the Umatilla Reservation (CTUIR), the First Nations Development Institute, and the Northwest Renewable

Resources Center. The CTUIR had recently embarked on their new Nations Project whereby the Tribes were seeking to restore their original treaty homeland, and to address issues related to their allotted lands. They thought the best way to do this would be to network with other tribes who were in a similar situation and consequently organized the First Indian Land Symposium.

The Indian Land Working Group (ILWG) was an outgrowth of this first symposium, where attendees decided that the tribes and Indian individuals should continue to share their knowledge and ideas on how to address problems stemming from mixed (Indian and non-Indian) land ownership of Indian homelands. The over 150 conference attendees moved to form the ILWG, which today continues to conduct the annual symposiums.

In addition to the symposium, the ILWG: conducts workshops and meetings related to land issues throughout the year, has produced an Indian Land Consolidation Manual, developed a draft legislative proposal which addresses land issues related to estate planning, data development, real estate transactions, acquisition financing, and Native American probate; and has produced a series of educational videos which seek to empower tribes and Native American landowner by sharing strategies related to recovery, consolidation, use and preservation of allotted homelands.

Prior to the Allotment Act tribal land holdings totaled 138 million acres. By the end of the allotment period in 1934, nearly 90 million acres held passed out of Native tribal ownership.

How many reservations are allotted?

There is approximately 11 million acres of allotted land on 100 reservations effecting some 300,000 allottees.

Who lives on reservations?

Today, most reservations have non-Natives residents and landowners living within the boundaries of reservations.

- ❖ 11 million acres (20%) within reservation boundaries are owned by non-Native Americans.
- ❖ Nearly one-half (46%) of the reservation population are non-Native Americans.

BUREAU OF INDIAN AFFAIRS (BIA)

The following excerpt is from the BIA website in their own words.

A Short History

While the Bureau of Indian Affairs did not receive congressional authorization until 1834, ten years after it had been administratively established by the Secretary of War, the stage was set for its creation in the earliest days of the U.S. government. One of the first actions taken by the Continental Congress in 1775 was to name a Committee on Indian Affairs. The committee established three departments of Indian Affairs and called upon such prominent Americans as Benjamin Franklin and Patrick Henry to assume leadership roles in the operation of these offices.

Henry Knox, Secretary of War, assumed responsibility for Indian affairs with the ordinance of August 7, 1786. The first Congress continued administration of Indian affairs within the War Department, established in 1789, with direction to the Secretary to place armed militia at the disposal of Indian commissioners "for negotiating treaties with the Indians."

Trading houses were maintained from 1786 to 1822 to supply Indians with necessary goods and, in exchange, to offer them a fair price for their furs. This was a matter of importance and concern for the government. As a result, the office of Superintendent of Trade was created in 1806 to place some controls on the practice of trading with Indians.

Without authorization from Congress, Secretary of War John C. Calhoun on March 11, 1824, created what he called the Bureau of Indian Affairs. The logical choice to head this office was Thomas McKenny, who had been Superintendent of Trade when that post was abolished two years earlier.

The matter of giving its approval to the establishment of an Indian office was vigorously debated in the Congress. But before such a measure was passed, the lawmakers created the position of Commissioner of Indian Affairs.

On July 9, 1832, Congress authorized the President "to appoint by and with the advice and consent of the Senate, a Commissioner of Indian Affairs, who shall, under the direction of the Secretary of War, and agreeable to such regulations as the President may, from time to time, prescribe, have the direction and management of all Indian affairs, and of all matters arising out of Indian relations."

The first presidentially appointed Commissioner was Elbert Herring. His salary was set at $3,000 per year.

In the first session of the 23rd Congress in 1834, the Committee on Indian Affairs of the House of Representatives produced three bills dealing with Indian affairs. These included measures to (1) organize a Department of Indian Affairs, (2) regulated trade with Indians, and (3) provide for the establishment of a western territory in which the Indians should be separated.

The third measure did not pass, but the other two were enacted into law. On June 30, 1834, the Bureau of Indian Affairs came into being through what has since become known as the organic law of the Indian office.

The organizational structure of Indian affairs during the 1800s primarily included two types of field jurisdictions, superintendents and agents. The superintendents were generally responsible for Indian affairs within a geographical area, usually a territory. Agents, some reporting to superintendents and others directly to the Indian affairs office, were concerned with the affairs of one or more tribes.

The Bureau of Indian Affairs was to remain in the War Department for 15 years after its creation by Congress. An act on March 3, 1849, established the Home Department of the Interior and Indian affairs passed from military to civilian control.

Development of the reservation system gained momentum in the mid-1850s after experimentation with the reservation policy in California. The role of the Bureau changed in the last quarter of the 1800s and specialized activities such as irrigation, forestry, Indian employment, law enforcement, health, and construction became increasingly more important.

Education of young Indians came to the forefront in 1879, when the first off-reservation boarding school was established at Carlisle, Pennsylvania. Chemwa Indian School in Oregon, Haskell Institute in Kansas, and Chilocco Indian School in Oklahoma were opened within the next five years. Other schools were to follow.

After World War II, a system of area offices was established and area directors were made responsible for administering all Indian programs within their geographical locations. This three-tier structure continues today, with organizational lines extending from Washington, DC to the area offices to the agencies at the reservation level.

Until 1973, the Bureau of Indian Affairs was placed organizationally under an Interior Department assistant secretary whose principle responsibilities revolved around land and water resources or other Interior programs. Indian affairs was a secondary concern of this official and frequently Indian goals and objectives were opposed by other Interior agencies.

This situation was partially corrected when Morris Thompson became Commissioner in 1973 and was made directly responsible to the Secretary of the Interior.

Finally, in 1977, the post of Assistant Secretary of Indian Affairs was created, thereby assuring the Bureau of a voice in policy matters within the Interior Department. Forrest Gerard, a member of the Blackfeet Indian tribe, became the first to fill this office.

Mission Statement

The Bureau of Indian Affairs' mission is to enhance the quality of life, to promote economic opportunity, and to carry out the responsibility to protect and improve the trust assets of American

Indians, Indian tribes and Alaska Natives. We will accomplish this through the delivery of quality services, maintaining government-to-government relationships within the spirit of Indian self-determination.

Vision Statement

The Bureau of Indian Affairs is a challenging and dynamic place to work. We provide high quality services in a timely and professional manner. We have the organizational flexibility to meet the changing needs of our customers. Our employees are committed, knowledgeable and empowered. Our polices are clear, consistent and supported throughout the organization. We manage for excellence, fostering cooperation and coordination in consultation with Indian Tribes while supporting self-determination and tribal sovereignty.

Trust responsibility

The following is an excerpt from the American Indian Policy & Research Institute. They have defined the Trust responsibility as well as it can be stated.

"The progress that the tribes made in the last 50 years is rolling back to the '50s where people are talking about terminating Indian tribes. The conscience of the dominant society has changed," said Bobby White-feather, Red Lake tribal chairman, in opening discussion of the relationship between the federal government and Indian tribes.

The United States Constitution, which is patterned after the Great Law of the Iroquois Confederacy, recognized Indian tribes as sovereign nations. During the colonial period and the infancy of the United States, tribes exerted great influence on the Europeans living in North

The United States Constitution, which is patterned after the Great Law of the Iroquois Confederacy, recognized Indian tribes as sovereign nations.

America. Tribes were considered military and political equals, and were often key allies in power struggles between the colonies and the Old World countries.

However, when the military power of Indian nations waned, some people in the United States began to view them as subservient even though the legal nation to nation relationship remained the same.

As late as the 1830s, the Supreme Court recognized that the relationship between Indian tribes and the United States was that of one nation to another. This relationship did not involve states or local governments. In fact, in Worchester v. Georgia, the Supreme Court ruled that because of the nationhood of the Cherokee Tribe, the laws of Georgia could have no force on them.

"The words 'treaty' and 'nation' are words of our own language, selected in our diplomatic and legislative proceedings, by ourselves, having each a definite and well understood meaning. We have applied them to Indians, as we have applied them to the other nations of the earth. They are applied to all in the same sense," writes the Supreme Court.

What has changed in the twentieth century is not the legal relationship between United States and Indian tribes, but rather the perspective. As the United States followed Manifest Destiny westward consuming land and resources, tribes began to be looked upon as dependent domestic nations instead of as foreign nations. As domestic nations within another nation, the federal government has a responsibility to protect the interests of Indians.

"The trust relationship evolved judicially and survived occasional congressional attempts to terminate the gov-

ernment's obligations to Indians. In theory, the trust relationship exists to protect tribes and individual Indians.
However, in practice, the federal trustee has at times not
worked in the best interests of the intended beneficiar-
ies," according to attorney Larry Leventhal, writing for the
Hamline Law Review. One way to conceptualize trust
responsibility is to think of it as treaty responsibility, said
Dennis King, an Oglala tribal council member. The federal government still has the responsibility to honor
agreements and treaties, which is why it is important for
Indians to be knowledgeable about the treaties that
affect them.

Often the promises made by the United States in
treaties are enforceable under the trust doctrine. In a
1983 decision, United States v. Mitchell, the Supreme
Court developed a standard for determining liability arising from a breach of trust responsibility.

It's important to note that although federal trust
responsibility arises out a the nationhood of tribes, the
trust doctrine also applies to individual Indians. This is
unlike sovereignty and sovereign immunity, which can
only be applied to nations.

The American Indian Policy Review Commission, set
up by Congress in 1975, called federal trust responsibility
the most important as well as the most misunderstood
concept in Federal-Indian relations.

Part of the misunderstanding may stem from actions of
Congress. The federal government has often acted inconsistently with and in opposition to the principles of trust
doctrine, leaving the public and many tribes confused.

The AIPRC defined the United States as a fiduciary
whose actions were to be judged by the highest standards. Because the federal government has so much

> *What has changed in the twentieth century is not the legal relationship between United States and Indian tribes, but rather the perspective.*

The federal government has often acted inconsistently with and in opposition to the principles of trust doctrine, leaving the public and many tribes confused.

control over the resources of Indian nations and individual Indians, the trust doctrine is implied in dealings even if not implicitly stated.

Trust responsibility affects everything the federal government is involved in, from education and health care to trust lands and the Bureau of Indian Affairs.

In his term in office, President Bill Clinton acknowledged the broad trust responsibility of the federal government. In an Executive Memorandum, he directed all cabinet heads and departments to work with tribes in a government-to-government relationship.

Trust responsibility has come under challenge by Congress as budget cuts have reduced services guaranteed to tribes through treaties. "When things are not going well, the federal government wants out from under trust responsibility," Whitefeather said.

Public attention has focused on a small number of tribes that have been visibly successful through casino gambling. Public perception tends to lump all tribes into that same category. Clearly there is a need for more public awareness of the legal and political framework that has shaped federal-tribal relations.

Many Indians have been re-examining trust responsibility too, and finding that the federal government has not lived up to its principles. In just one example, the Bureau of Indian Affairs mismanagement and complete lack of accounting of funds has resulted in the disappearance of $2.4 billion dollars of Indian money.

BIA — Friend or Foe?

Native American issues are mired in a morass of demographics complicated by convoluted tribalism:

❖ Nearly 2.4 million self-declared Native Americans.

❖ Approximately 1.4 million enrolled tribal members.

❖ 559 Federally-recognized tribes.

❖ 150 different languages and dialects.

❖ 314 Federally-recognized reservations.

❖ 40+ State-recognized reservations.

The monumental task of administration and management of this demographic nightmare is the responsibility of the Bureau of Indian Affairs. During its 176 year history, the BIA has often been the subject of severe criticism in the execution of its responsibilities on behalf of American Indians.

The BIA and Native Americans are diametrically opposed philosophically. The BIA has the trust responsibility to ensure that tribes receive their lawful treaty entitlements in the form of special programs; and on the other hand and at the same time encourage self-determination and independence as domestic sovereign nations.

It's a "Catch 22." On one hand the BIA is the pipeline for Federal programs and on the other hand they interfere and exert too much government control over sovereign Tribal affairs. Is it time for BIA reform or should the BIA be phased out and true tribal sovereignty exercised? Is "dependent sovereign" an oxymoron?

The BIA is not the enemy. In fairness to the BIA today, it should be understood that, in 176 years, many past sins and much of the chaos was institutionalized and inherited. I personally know and have worked with BIA personnel that are capable and dedicated people. The BIA has been and still is a tremendous resource for Native Americans.

How much do BIA programs cost?

The federal government spends about $8 billion annually on Native American programs.

> *Public attention has focused on a small number of tribes that have been visibly successful through casino gambling.*

75

Is "dependent sovereign" an oxymoron?

The following is President Clinton's proposed 2000 BIA budget.

President Clinton has submitted a final budget proposal asking for a total of $9.4 billion for new and existing Native American programs — an increase of $1.2 billion. Native American officials believe they can get both political parties to support the president's budget for the largest increase in Native American country funding.

Details of the president's proposed budget for tribes were released the second week in February. The president is asking for $300 million for BIA school construction and repair; $349 million through the Department of Transportation for roads in Native American country; $2.6 billion for the Native American Health Service (IHS), an increase of $230 million; $439 million for the departments of Justice and Interior, an increase of $103 million. The initiative will improve public safety for the over 1.4 million residents on the approximately 56 million acres of Native American lands.

The administration is also proposing $108 million toward cleaning up trust fund accounts that have been mismanaged for the past 100 years. The trust reform request would nearly double this year's clean-up budget.

Supporting tribal self-determination is another aspect of the Clinton budget. Under the administration's proposal, the BIA and IHS will continue to promote tribal self-determination through local decision-making. Tribal contracting and self-governance compact agreements now represent 41 percent of BIA's operations budget, and forty-two percent of IHS' budget. The self-governance agreements give tribes greater flexibility to administer federal programs on reservations.

Within the overall BIA increase, the budget proposal

includes $134 million, a $9 million or seven percent increase over 2000 for contract support costs. This funding provides $5 million for new and expanded contracts and $129 million for existing contracts.

And where it is estimated that more than 100,000 Native Americans are in need of decent homes, the administration is proposing $650 million in block grants for Native American housing, an increase of $30 million, and $32 million to repair or replace dilapidated homes. The budget proposes to set aside $5 million within the Native American Housing Block Grant to create non-profit homeownership intermediaries in Native American country. They would serve as a catalyst for the creation of a private homeownership market, and would support local capacity-building intermediaries or "one-stop mortgage centers."

But even this proposed largest fiscal increase in tribal history is not enough to meet all the needs. For instance, currently there is an $800 million backlog in school repairs and construction. And there is a $700 million backlog in transportation needs, as well.

The president's budget calls for encouraging economic growth on reservations. Under the administration's plan to build new markets in the nation, he is proposing a plan to initiate new business development in Native American country, as well.

The president is seeking $4.5 million to create small business development centers that would provide technical business and technical assistance to Native American entrepreneurs. And the president's economic plan for tribes includes encouraging businesses to invest in creating a Native American labor workforce.

Tribal contracting and self-governance compact agreements now represent 41 percent of BIA's operations budget, and forty-two percent of IHS' budget.

77

Notes:

_____

_____

_____

_____

_____

_____

_____

_____

_____

_____

_____

_____

_____

"Two years ago I made an unscheduled visit to the town of Guadalupe, Arizona, home to 5,600 people of Hispanic and Yaqui Native American descent. The Third World conditions there — unpaved roads, dilapidated housing high unemployment — made an indelible impression on me. I vowed to do all in my power to bring hope and opportunity to Guadalupe and other economic disaster areas like it across America."

— Secretary of HUD
Jack Kemp, July 1992

Third World conditions are still the reality for most of Native America and they are still the poorest race of people in the country with regard to health, education and welfare. The prosperity of a handful of hugely successfully gaming tribes has eclipsed the grinding poverty of the vast majority of Native Americans.

Section 3:
The Facts of Life

As ludicrous as it may sound, Native Americans were categorically granted United States citizenship by the 1924 Indian Citizenship Act.

Are Native Americans US citizens?

As ludicrous as it may sound, Native Americans were categorically granted United States citizenship by the 1924 Indian Citizenship Act. Citizenship had been conferred upon approximately two-thirds of the Indian population through treaty agreements, statutes, naturalization proceedings, and by service in the Armed Forces with an honorable discharge in World War I.

With citizenship came all rights and obligations of any other United States citizens. Theoretically, enrolled tribal members have dual citizenship.

Do Native Americans serve in the armed forces?

Yes. Indians have the same obligations for military service as other U.S. citizens. They have fought in all American wars since the Revolution.

In the Civil War, they served on both sides. Eli S. Parker, Seneca from New York, was at Appomattox as aide to Gen. Ulysses S. Grant when Lee surrendered, and the unit of Confederate Brigadier General Stand Watie (Cherokee) was the last to surrender.

During World War I, Native Americans demonstrated patriotism (6,000 of the more than 8,000 who served were volunteers) moved Congress to pass the Indian Citizenship Act of 1924.

During World War II, 25,000 Indian men and women, mainly enlisted Army personnel, fought on all fronts in Europe and Asia, winning (according to an incomplete count) 71 Air Medals, 51 Silver Stars, 47 Bronze Stars, 34 Distinguished Flying Crosses, and two Congressional Medals of Honor. The most famous Indian exploit of World War II was the use by Navajo Marines of their language as a battlefield code, the only such code that the enemy could not break.

In the Korean conflict, there was one Indian Congressional Medal of Honor winner.

In the Vietnam War, 41,500 Indians served in the military forces.

In 1990, prior to Operation Desert Storm, some 24,000 Indian men and women were in the military.

Approximately 3,000 served in the Persian Gulf with three among those killed in action.

One out of every four Indian males is a military veteran and approximately 50 percent of tribal leaders today are military veterans.

Are treaties still made with Native tribes?

No. The first treaty was made with the Delawares in 1778 and in 1871 Congress declared that no Indian nation would be recognized for the purpose of making treaties. Since then, relations with Indian groups are by Congressional Acts, Executive Orders, and Executive Agreements. Between 1778 and 1871, the U.S. Senate ratified 370 Indian treaties. At least 45 others were negotiated with tribes but were never ratified by the Senate.

Originals of all the treaties are maintained by the National Archives and Records Service of the General Services Administration. A duplicate of a treaty is available upon request for a fee. The agency will also answer questions about specific Indian treaties. Write to: Diplomatic Branch, National Archives and Records Services, Washington, DC 20408

What are tribal treaty entitlements?

Any special rights that Native tribes or members of those tribes have are generally based on treaties or other agreements between the United States and tribes. Native tribes paid a heavy price to retain certain "sovereign" rights and entitlements by relinquishing much of their land to the United States.

The inherent rights they did not relinquish are protected by U.S. law. Among those may be hunting and fishing rights and access to religious sites

Any special rights that Native tribes or members of those tribes have are generally based on treaties or other agreements between the United States and tribes.

Do Native Americans get monthly government checks?

No individual is automatically paid for being a Native American. The Federal Government may pay a tribe or an individual in compensation for damages for losses resulting from treaty violations, for encroachments on Indian lands, or for other past or present wrongs.

A tribe or an individual may also receive a government check for payment of income from their lands and resources. This occurs because their resources are held in trust by the Secretary of the Interior and payment for their use has been collected from users by the Federal Government in their behalf. Fees collected from oil or grazing leases are an example of this situation.

Some 47 tribes that have successful casinos pay "per capita" checks to members after social programs are funded and tribal infrastructures have been built.

Do Native Americans get a free college education?

No. An individual does not automatically receive funding because of Native American ancestry. The Native American higher education program provides financial aid to eligible students, based on demonstrated financial need, who have plans to attend an accredited institution of higher education.

A student must obtain an application packet and other financial aid information form their tribe, home BIA Agency, or Area Office of Indian Education Programs. The Higher Education Grant Program is available to an individual who is a member of a federally recognized Native American tribe.

Some tribes that have successful casinos offer to provide a college education for tribal members.

THE NATIVE AMERICAN CONDITION

Health

The Indian Health Service (IHS) is the principal Federal health care provider and health advocate for American Indian/Alaska Native people, and its goal is to raise their health status to the highest possible level. The IHS currently provides health services to approximately 1.4 million American Indians and Alaska Natives who belong to more that 559 federally recognized tribes in 34 states.

The IHS administers a health care system for American Indians/Alaska Natives that includes 49 hospitals in 12 states, 180 health centers in 27 states, and eight school health centers and 273 health stations in 18 states. The health care system is operated through the cooperative efforts of Federal and American Indian and Alaska Native entities.

The IHS has some 15,000 employees.

The following statistics are from the Regional Differences in Indian Health 1998–1999:

❖ Alcohol mortality is 627% greater than for all other races combined.

❖ Tuberculosis is 533% greater than all other Americans.

❖ Diabetes is 6.8 times greater than all other Americans.

❖ Fetal Alcohol Syndrome (FAS) is 33 times higher than other Americans.

❖ One in six adolescents has attempted suicide — four times that of all other teenagers.

❖ Pneumonia and influenza is 61% greater than all other Americans.

❖ Homicide is 63% greater than all other Americans.

Education

"Education is your most powerful weapon. With education you are the white mans equal; without education you are his victim, and so shall remain all your lives. Study, learn, help one another always. Remember there is only poverty and misery in idleness and dreams – but in work there is self respect and independence."

— Chief Plenty Coups, Crow Tribe

BIA funds 187 schools on 63 reservations located in 23 states. In all, about 50,000 Native American students are served in Bureau funded schools. At present more than half of the schools are operated through grants to Tribes and local school boards.

The lack of internet access is a major concern for the BIA school system.

Student performance and participation is far below the national average:

❖ 52% finish high school.
❖ 17% attend college.
❖ 4% graduate from college.
❖ 2% attend graduate school.

Why Native Peoples Are At Risk

Our schools have failed to nurture the intellectual development and academic performance of many native children, as is evident from their high dropout rates and negative attitudes toward school.

Our schools have discouraged the use of Native languages in the classroom, thereby contributing to a weakening of the Natives' resolve to retain and continue the development of their original languages and cultures.

Native American lands and resources are constantly besieged by outside forces interested in further reducing their original holdings.

Political relationships between the tribes and the federal government fluctuate with the will of this U.S. Congress and decisions by the courts.

— Excerpt from the U S Dept. of Education
"Native American Nations At Risk Task Force", 1991

Economically

Native Americans are disadvantaged in the development of business acumen as entrepreneurs. The disparity between the income of Native Americans and mainstream economics is widening in direct proportion to their lack of experience, opportunity and resources. From a historical perspective, Native Americans are recent arrivals to the political and economic arena.

❖ 75% of the work force earn less than $7,000 per year.

❖ 45% are below the poverty level.

❖ The average unemployment rate is 45%.

❖ Unemployment on some reservations is 90%.

Most housing is inadequate and substandard. For instance, Navajos, who have the largest reservation and tribe with the most resources, endure the following conditions:

❖ 46% have no electricity.

❖ 54% have no indoor plumbing.

❖ 82% live without a telephone.

These Third World living conditions are typical of most reservation communities. Poor health care, miserable poverty and substandard education are a daily fact of life for most Native Americans.

85

"During 1992, we will honor this country's native peoples as vital participants in the history of the United States. This year gives us the opportunity to recognize the special place that Native Americans hold in our society, to affirm the right of Native American tribes to exist as sovereign entities and to seek greater mutual understanding and trust."
— President George Bush, March 1992

"Two years ago I made an unscheduled visit to the town of Guadalupe, AZ, home to 5,600 people of Hispanic and Yaqui Native American descent. The Third World conditions there — unpaved roads, dilapidated housing high unemployment — made an indelible impression on me. I vowed to do all in my power to bring hope and opportunity to Guadalupe and other economic disaster areas like it across America."
— Secretary of HUD Jack Kemp,
July 1992

"During 1992, we will honor this country's native peoples as vital participants in the history of the United States. This year gives us the opportunity to recognize the special place that Native Americans hold in our society, to affirm the right of Native American tribes to exist as sovereign entities and to seek greater mutual understanding and trust."
— President George Bush,
March 1992

"Indian Tribes should be subject to state law. My view is that state law reigns supreme when it comes to the Indians, whether it be gambling or any other issue,"
— Gov. George Bush, Jr. (R-TX)
Presidential candidate, 1999

Native Americans have made sporadic uprisings that receive brief notoriety and media exposure. However, as public and political attention wanes, it is business as usual. An objective evaluation of the Native American condition would conclude that systems and programs employed for the last 100 years are not working very well.

The most effective strategy to incapacitate and destroy any organization is by internal dissention. Native Americans are particularly vulnerable to this strategy because of egocentric tribalism. They have been divided historically by circumstance and design.

Reality Check

The United States is outraged at oppression and abuse of indigenous people in other countries, while at home Native Americans are a dispossessed and disenfranchised people in their own homeland. The hypocrisy should be an embarrassment to the country that is considered the world leader of democracy and guardian of human rights. It is incumbent upon the United States government to set an example for the world with regard to treatment of their respective native inhabitants.

Almost everyone agrees that Native Americans have legitimate grievances that have not been equitably resolved, however, most Native American issues are obscured by current national and international crises.

To establish a realistic perspective, list some of the country's major domestic and foreign problems. Rank them in some order of priority:

AIDS
Third world starvation
Homelessness
Drug problems
Education
Health care
Social Security
Space programs
Military defense
Environmental pollution

The list is endless. Now rank Native American issues on that list.

As Senator DeConcini of Arizona so aptly stated from a congressional perspective: "Nobody gives a damn about Indians."

Congress is the political and economic power base of the country and Congress is motivated by a combination of politics, economics, public opinion and lobbied interests. There are few Native American advocates in Congress. As Senator DeConcini of Arizona so aptly stated from a congressional perspective: "Nobody gives a damn about Indians."

Although major Native American civilizations had flourished centuries before the white man's arrival, Native American cultures were not recognized by Europeans as established civilizations. Nor have they been given the appropriate recognition for their significant contributions to the development of this country.

Native American issues are emotionally charged and logic is often clouded by the heat of the moment. It is very difficult to be objective. Attitude and the law are often a matter of convenience and purpose as the United States government justifies its treatment of Native Americans.

The dilemma is compounded by social complacency and misinformation. Negative stereotyping is still prevalent today and serves as an effective conduit for discrimination and prejudice that lead to exploitation. Neither attitudes nor morality can be legislated; they can only be formed through education.

Adaptability is fundamental to most Native American problems. Native Americans are polarized between tradition and culture on one hand and adaptation to the progress of the dominant culture on the other. The issue seems to be the appropriate degree of adaptability.

Obviously, a lesser degree of adaptability is required from a Navajo sheepherder or an artist living a traditional lifestyle on the reservation than from a Navajo attorney or a business person living in the Phoenix metro area.

Even traditional reservation Native Americans have adapted to one degree or another. Horses, guns and clothing were early adaptations. Modern home construction, electricity, running water, automobiles, television and phones are evidence of more recent adaptation.

Being Native American is not just a matter of blood quantum, it is a state of being and a spirituality. Traditionally, Native American spirituality is an integral part of daily living in harmony with the rhythms of nature.

Historically, most Native American tribes were primarily a migratory people. The migrations were dictated by the laws of nature and more recently, by the mandates of the dominant society. A cultural consequence of these migrations is an attachment of spiritual significance to geographic features.

Each Urban Native American must determine what degree of adaptation is required to function as a productive member of society and yet preserve their Native American connections. Some Native Americans wear long hair, braids, jewelry and apparel as a declaration, while others use some or none of the trappings.

Nothing is forever and the only thing for sure is change. Native Americans are a very small minority (less than 1% of the US population) who are a step behind mainstream society by all socio-economic standards. They are clinging to a past-life that may be morally and ecologically correct. However, change is the natural order of things and life moves on.

Each Urban Native American must determine what degree of adaptation is required to function as a productive member of society and yet preserve their Native American connections.

Notes:

_____

_____

_____

_____

_____

_____

_____

_____

_____

_____

_____

_____

Public empathy toward Native American issues will diminish with each succeeding generation. Today's generation will not assume the sins of their forefathers. Too much time has passed and there are too many contemporary issues that have a higher priority.

Native America's destiny is at a crossroads. Native Americans must prepare to take control of their destiny, as gently as possible. The next battles will be won by attorneys whose weapons are the legal briefs and laptop computers. The skirmishes will be fought in courtrooms and political battles waged in Congressional committees.

Section 4:
The Future

The fault dear Brutus, lies not in our stars but within ourselves.

— William Shakespeare, *Julius Caesar*

STRATEGIC PLANNING

Do Tribes have a Plan for Self-Determination?

Native Americans are survivors. They have survived 400 years of genocide and 100 years of BIA dominance and government control. They have a strong spirituality closely tied to the land, and their religions reflect a respect for the mysterious powers of nature. For the moment, it appears that the pendulum of social conscience has swung in favor of the Native Americans. People of conscience are empathetic to the plight of Native Americans. In the academic community there are concerted efforts to include a more accurate account of Native American history and culture.

Empathy is wonderful, however, the time has come for Native Americans to take control of their own destiny. Historically, when political and economic forces covet Native American land and resources, social conscience is compromised. Avarice has the inherent ability to justify and rationalize its actions. The ends justify the means. The goals can now be accomplished through clever paper and political manipulations, rather than the overt physical aggressions of the past.

The idea that Native people can live in tranquil harmony with nature on reservations is a dangerous illusion. Today's Native Americans cannot walk the path of their ancestors. The last bargaining chip is the reservations and their respective resources. Native Americans must take appropriate precautions to protect those remaining resources.

For thousands of years, tribalism was an instinct that was necessary for survival. Tribalism has an up side and a down side. The up side is that tribalism is a source of Native American strength, culture and tradition. The down side is that tribalism has always been at the heart of Native American dissension.

Historically, when political and economic forces covet Native American land and resources, social conscience is compromised.

Egocentric tribalism is not conducive to the development of significant national political or economic power. Democracy is a game of numbers, and the majority rules. Of the 2 million self-declared Native Americans in the country approximately 1.4 million are enrolled. The enrolled Native American population is less than ½ of 1% of the total population of 278 million!

Nearly all reservation lands are held in "trust" by the US government. The Congressional fox is guarding the Native American chicken coop.

- ❖ 11 million acres (20%) within reservation boundaries are owned by non-Native Americans.
- ❖ Nearly one-half (46%) of the reservation population are non-Native Americans.
- ❖ Less than 10% of contemporary Native Americans speak their native language.
- ❖ Native Americans continue to be a political embarrassment and an economic thorn in the side of federal and state governments.

Why Do Native Americans have a PR problem?

Spearheaded by pulp novels and western movies, Native Americans became a blur of monosyllabic drunken savages, living in teepees, usually in a feathered headdress with warpaint, dancing and whooping around a fire. They were the hapless victims of a one-sided media campaign that relentlessly created stereotypical images primarily for entertainment. The character assassination was complete to the last detail. America embraced the fictional image to the extent that new myths were based on old myths.

As a result, the Native American has been relegated to the past, the villainous savages in John Wayne movies, comedic trivialization, or worse, as sports teams and their mascots. Time and technology have desensitized America and provided a convenient immunization to a dark page in America's history.

Nearly all reservation lands are held in "trust" by the US government. The Congressional fox is guarding the Native American chicken coop.

93

America's conscience has been appeased with regard to the Native American condition by misinformation, disinformation and complacency

Psychologically, a less-than-human Native American image was necessary to sanction conquest and soothe the nation's moral conscience. The best image Native Americans could hope for was a "Tonto" or "Little Beaver," as trusted companions to their superior white counterparts.

America's conscience has been appeased with regard to the Native American condition by misinformation, disinformation and complacency. Contemporary Native Americans have become invisible in the mind's eye of the nation's moral conscience. When there is reference to minorities, the focus is on African-Americans, Hispanics, Asians and "others." Native Americans are usually included among the "others."

Native Americans must shoulder their share of responsibility for conduct that has contributed to their negative image. It is the responsibility of the Native American community to replace that negative image with a more accurate and positive image.

Native Americans had 2 important characteristics in days of old:

❖ They were the great athletes; before the horse, Native people traveled by foot. They were great long-distance runners and superb hunters. The diet was lean.
❖ They were great storytellers and eloquent orators: Native people did not essentially have written languages or records, although some tribes developed pictographs and petroglyphs.

Native tribes have contributed immensely to the plagiarism of certain culture, traditions and ceremonies by public display at pow wows. The public is invited and coyly asked not to take pictures of certain sacred ceremonies. Perhaps there should be public pow wows and private pow wows, each with its own agenda and purpose.

Can we realistically expect today's society to be compassionate about Native American problems? Today's society is oblivious to memories of the Great Depression, World Wars I and II, and has only fading memories of Vietnam and Civil Rights marches of the 60's. They are certainly not concerned with atrocities perpetrated generations before they were born. Today's generation will not assume the sins of their forefathers.

There are literally hundreds of programs, agencies, organizations and publications that are concerned with Native American issues. The effective entities must develop a centralized communication system that nurtures interaction and networking. The Internet is a window of opportunity for Native Americans to make a quantum leap in networking and communication.

Today's generation will not assume the sins of their forefathers.

Is it time to assume responsibility?

Native Americans can no longer rely on the "big brother" paternalistic benevolence of the US government. Government subsidies for necessities of life are not the answer to Native American future. The answers are education, political unity and economic independence.

POLITICAL POWER

Do Tribes have political Clout?

Ben Nighthorse Campbell (R-CO) is the only Native American in Congress. Native Americans do not have collective political clout. They must deal with the fact that a divided people are a vulnerable and manageable people. Remember Senator DeConcini's comment: "Nobody gives a damn about Indians."

For the first time in history, gaming tribes have the resources and are beginning to flex their political money muscles by political contributions to candidates who are advocates for their agenda. And by the same token, they are launching a political campaign offensive against opponents such as long-time nemesis Senator Slade Gorton (R-WA).

War may be too strong a word, but the Native American people and their lands are essentially under siege. They are in a battle for survival.

Can Native Americans vote?

Indians have the same right to vote as other U.S. citizens.

❖ In 1948, the Arizona Supreme Court declared as unconstitutional disenfranchising interpretation of the State constitution and allowed Native people to vote.

❖ In 1953, a Utah State law stated that persons living on Native tribal reservations were not residents of the State and could not vote, was repealed.

❖ In 1954, Native tribes in Maine who were not then Federally-recognized, were given the right to vote.

❖ In 1962, New Mexico extended the right to vote to Native people.

Do Native Americans vote?

Native Americans are notorious for their lack of participation in the political process. Estimates are as low as 10% voter turnout in past elections. Most Native Americans feel that the political process is a white man's game, and they traditionally do not participate.

War may be too strong a word, but the Native American people and their lands are essentially under siege. They are in a battle for survival. It's a different kind of cold war that's insidious by nature and nurtured by apathy. In order for Native Americans to survive, they must view each election as a battle.

Each Native American vote is an arrow. Each time a Native American doesn't vote, it's the same as a vote for the opposition. If Native Americans do not participate in the decision making political process by voting, then other interest groups, with their own agendas, will make those decisions for them.

Politicians respond to votes. If an important Native American issue is presented to the Congressional Committee on Indian Affairs, and the Chair of the Committee opens his door on a Monday morning to find 10,000 Native people faxes or emails — it would have a tremendous impact on the decision-making process.

And it is possible!

As of January 1, 1996, most US citizens can to register to vote by mail. A new national voter-registration form has been designed to make it more convenient for Americans to register for the first time or to make a change of address, name or political party.

Citizens can request the form from their state election officials, usually by phone, and use it to register to vote in all but five states: Arkansas, Virginia, New Hampshire (where it will only be accepted as a mail-in registration form for absentee voters), North Dakota (which does not require voters to register), and Wyoming, that will not permit the form's use.

Native Americans are not the only non-voters. In an embarrassing example to the world's other democracies, only 38.7% of all US citizens of voting age bothered to exercise their right and responsibility in the last national elections.

In 1994, the Navajo tribal election and the general election were on the same day and polling places were side by side. This made it easy for Navajo voters to choose their state and federal representatives.

Voter registration should be a requirement for enrollment. The Saginaw Chippewa's require voter registration for tribal voting and elections. They could both be done at the same time.

In those areas that have a large Native American population, particularly in the West, Native American groups are finding that they do have the power to influence the outcome of major elections. Native American voters are beginning to flex their political muscle.

Do Native Americans hold public office?

U.S. Senate:
❖ Hiram R. Revels, Lumbee from Mississippi, 1870–1871
❖ Mathew Stanley Quay, Abenaki or Delaware from Pennsylvania, 1887–1899 and 1901–1904

❖ Charles Curtis, Kaw from Kansas, 1907–1912 and 1915–1929 (Vice-President from 1929–1933)
❖ Robert L. Owens, Cherokee from Oklahoma, 1907–1925
❖ Ben Nighthorse Campbell — Current Republican Senator from Colorado

U.S. House of Representatives:
❖ Charles Curtis, Kaw from Kansas, 1893–1907
❖ Charles D. Carter, Choctaw from Oklahoma, 1907–1927
❖ W. W. Hastings, Cherokee from Oklahoma, 1915–1921 and 1923–1935
❖ Will Rogers, Jr., Cherokee from California, 1943–1944
❖ William G. Stigler, Chocktaw from Oklahoma, 1944–1952
❖ Benjamin Reifel, Rosebud Sioux from South Dakota, 1961–1971
❖ Clem Rogers McSpadden, Cherokee from Oklahoma, 1972–1975

Indians also served in and now hold office in a number of State legislatures. Others currently hold or have held elected or appointive positions in State judiciary systems and in county and city governments including local school boards. Larry Echo Hawk, an enrolled member of the Pawnee Tribe, served as attorney general of Idaho from 1992 to 1994.

What's wrong with "squaw"?

Trappers, settlers and frontiersmen consorted with Native women and often took Native wives. The social attitude toward this practice was reflected by the term "squaw" and "squawman" with reference to Native women and their European male counterparts. Within the context of the times, the designation "squaw" and "squawman" may have had various connotations, but the derogatory meaning was always clear.

Over the attrition of time, the term "squaw" was commonly used as a generic reference to Native women, until it was recently revealed that "squaw" was an Algonquin word for the female genitalia.

The issue became a point of contention in the Native American community and especially with Native American women. So please do not make the mistake of calling a Native American woman a "squaw"!

What's wrong with "Redskins?"

The Washington "Redskins" would not survive a season as the Washington "Blackskins" or "Yellowskins" or "Brownskins." For some games a pig is painted red, a simulated Native tribal chief's war-bonnet is strapped to the pig's head and its ran around the field to incite fan frenzy. I wonder how the black players on the team and the fans would feel if the pig was painted black with an afro wig strapped on its head and ran around the field?

The infamous "tomahawk chop" and chanting is another example of mindless and thoughtless racism. These images are repeatedly broadcast over national television in living color!

Would the Cleveland "Wahoo" cartoon mascot survive a season as the Cleveland "Kikes" or the Cleveland "Chinks" or the Cleveland "Sambos" or the Cleveland "Wops"?

It is demeaning and racist to use cartoon caricatures and cultural symbolism of a race of people as professional or academic, sports team mascots. There are a zillion names and mascots that are not offensive and damaging to any race of people.

I'm sure that it was not the intent of most sports fans to be malicious or racist. However, the hurt and racism inflicted on Native people, especially the young, is still the same regardless of intent. To be this mindless and thoughtless in today's society is immoral, inappropriate and unconscionable.

This is another example of the lack of Native American political clout. If it were a black mascot, the NAACP would impose a Washington Redskins boycott in a New York minute.

Within the context of the times, the designation "squaw" and "squawman" may have had various connotations, but the derogatory meaning was always clear.

Almost all Native American arts and crafts retail stores and businesses are owned by non-Native people.

NATIVE AMERICAN BUSINESS

Do Native Americans own businesses?

According to the SBA, there are 102,000 Native American owned businesses in the United States. Approximately 20,000 of those business are on reservations. Native Americans are making the transition from supplier to entrepreneur as they prepare to make the quantum leap from the blanket to the boardroom.

Native American arts and crafts are a multi-million dollar business with domestic and global markets. The role of Native Americans in the marketplace has traditionally been as the supplier of arts and crafts products. Almost all Native American arts and crafts retail stores and businesses are owned by non-Native people.

Native American business organizations.

State and Regional Chambers of Commerce.
Arizona American Indian Chamber of Commerce.
Southern California American Indian Chamber of Commerce.
Rocky Mountain Indian Chamber of Commerce.
Norwest American Indian Chamber of Commerce.
Texas American Indian Chamber of Commerce.
Minnesota American Indian Chamber of Commerce.
Oklahoma American Indian Chamber of Commerce.
Wisconsin American Indian Chamber of Commerce

Native American Business Organizations.
National Center for American Indian Enterprise Development.
Native American Business Alliance.
National Indian Business Association.
Native American Business Connection.
Arizona Native American Economic Coalition.
Arizona American Indian Tourism Association.

Do Native Americans pay taxes?

Yes. They pay the same taxes as other citizens with the following exceptions:

❖ Federal income taxes are not levied on income from trust lands held for them by the United States;

❖ State income taxes are not paid on income earned on a Indian reservation;

❖ State sales taxes are not paid by Indians on transactions made on an Indian reservation;

❖ Local property taxes are not paid on reservation or trust land.

Are Native Tribes getting rich from casinos?

Gaming is the current economic and political issue in Native American country. The issue of Native American sovereignty hangs in the balance as Native Americans cautiously negotiate the maze of overlapping state and federal jurisdictions and control.

Casinos seem to be a quick-fix basis for cash flow — a short term solution for long-term problems. It is very difficult to argue with success; however, the jury is still out on the long-term ramifications of gaming on Native American social and economic development.

A handful of the Native American casinos, with smaller enrollments near large metro areas, are generating fantastic revenues and are distributing per capita payments. Theoretically and literally, some tribal members have become millionaires in a very short period of time. Most tribal casinos generate much more modest revenues.

This brings up a number of issues: Does this wealth translate into shared wealth with alienated or disconnected tribal members and their Urban Native American counterparts? What will be the attitude of the federal government and the public towards subsidy programs as the tribal coffers fill? Will there still be health, education and entitlement subsidy programs for tribal members who are considered millionaires?

Casinos seem to be a quick-fix basis for cash flow — a short term solution for long-term problems.

101

What will be the attitude of the federal government and the public towards subsidy programs as the tribal coffers fill?

What will be the attitude and reaction of adjacent non-Native American communities toward the Native American gaming bonanza? Will there be a saturation of the gaming market with a casino on every corner? Or will there be a backlash if casino money machines absorb too much discretionary income and gambling becomes a blight on society?

As of this printing, California voters passed Proposition 5 which technically allows California's 107 federally recognized tribes to open two casinos each. Some estimates indicate there could be as may as 113,000 slot machines in the state. There are about 130,000 slots in Las Vegas. It won't happen overnight, but California could eventually give Atlantic City and Las Vegas a run for their money. Democratic Gov. Gray Davis has already signed gaming compacts with some 60 tribes.

After years of failed government programs, Indian reservations are among the poorest communities in the United States; Shannon County Oglala Sioux Reservation in South Dakota is ranked lowest in the U.S. Indian unemployment is six times the national average, and Indian health, education and income statistics are among the worst in the country.

Indian gaming is providing a means to self-sufficiency for Tribal Nations, and is also creating jobs and economic activity in local non-Indian communities and states where tribal gaming operations are located.

Who Regulates Native Tribal gaming?

Indian land is not under State law unless a Federal law places it under State law. The Supreme Court held that even if a tribe is under State law the State gaming regulations do not apply on Indian trust land.

In 1988 Congress passed the Indian Gaming Regulatory Act. This law allows traditional Indian gaming as well as bingo, pull tabs, lotto, punch boards, tip jars, and certain card games on tribal land. However, it requires a Tribal/State compact for other forms of gaming such as cards or slot machines.

The National Indian Gaming Commission was established by Congress to develop regulations for Indian gaming. For more information contact the National Indian Gaming Commission, 9th., Floor, 1441 L Street, NW, Washington, DC 20005, (202) 632-7003.

Native Tribal Gaming Facts (National Indian Gaming Association Library and Resource Center)

Size of Industry:
❖ Total number of Federally recognized tribes: 559
❖ Number of tribal governments engaged in gaming (Class II or III): 198
❖ Just over one-third of the federally recognized tribes have gaming operations.
❖ Number of tribal gaming operations: 326
❖ Number states with tribal-state compacts: 28
❖ Number of tribal-state compacts: 198

Revenue:
❖ Indian gaming revenue in 1999: $8.26 billion (10% of total gaming industry)
❖ 22 tribal operations account for 56 % of the revenue
❖ 47 tribal governments give out per capita payments to tribal members

Employment:
❖ Total jobs in Indian gaming: 200,000
❖ Percentage of Indian to non-Indian: 75% non-Indian, 25% Indian

> *Native Americans have the responsibility, to those ancestors who fired arrows against cannons and survived against overwhelming odds, to make that survival meaningful.*

TEN YEAR AGENDA

Native Americans are a small but select minority who have the unique feature of millennial ties to this land. They are survivors with a common bond who have withstood 400 years of "ations:" extermination, termination and assimilation. Native Americans are survivors. Through all the trials and tribulations, they have sustained a sense of humor. Native Americans have lost most battles, but not the war.

Immigrants, of all races, come to this country with a worn suitcase and a dream. Ten years later, many are educated and prosperous. Are Native Americans any less capable? Native Americans have the responsibility, to those ancestors who fired arrows against cannons and survived against overwhelming odds, to make that survival meaningful.

It seems a basic requirement to study the history of our Native American people. America has much to learn about the heritage of our American Native Americans. Only through this study can we as a nation do what must be done if our treatment of the American Native American is not to be marked down for all time as a national disgrace.
— John F. Kennedy, 1963

Native Americans have had time and opportunity to help correct the course of their own destiny. They must divorce themselves from the "helpless victim" mindset that blames the government for their station in life. (Even if it's true.) The time has come for Native Americans to help themselves. All that life owes any of us is opportunity, and no one ever said that life was going to be fair.

Public empathy toward Native American issues will diminish with each succeeding generation. Today's generation will not, and probably should not, assume the sins of their forefathers. Too much time has passed and there are too many contemporary issues that have a higher priority.

Native Americans must prepare by education to take control of their destiny, as gently as possible. The next battles will be won by warriors in three-piece suits whose weapons are the briefcase and laptop computers. The skirmishes will be fought in courtrooms and battles won in Congressional committees.

Native American destiny is at a crossroads and the moment is at hand. Native Americans are a privileged people who want exclusivity. Native Americans are a special people, but they cannot be a separate people.

The only thing for sure in this life is change, and adaptability is an absolute for the survival of a species or a civilization. People lament for the "good old days," a time when life was simpler and basic values were solid. Sometime in the future, today will be someone's "good old days."

No one will argue against the importance of traditional values and lifestyles. But even traditions must evolve. I'm sure that what Native Americans consider traditional today is not the same as it was 500 years ago, 200 years ago or even 100 years ago. Most Native Americans had a seasonal migratory lifestyle and, in some cases, had to relocate because of droughts or other conditions beyond their control. When geography changes, so do traditions.

Times change. The younger generation of Native American women are no longer going to knead dough and cook frybread over an open fire outside the hogan. Nor are they going to sit cross-legged in front of a loom weaving a rug for 10 hours a day.

Not all traditions, cultural or religious, were good. In the light of today's knowledge, some were funny, some were dumb, and some were barbaric and cruel.

The very best time of your life is right now. Not yesterday when life was simpler. Not tomorrow when life will be easier. We are part

> *The only thing for sure in this life is change, and adaptability is an absolute for the survival of a species or a civilization.*

of the most exciting time in history with more opportunities than ever before. Of course there are problems, there always have been and there always will be.

We are all a work in progresss. That's what life is all about. Life is a learning experience from crib to coffin. An evolutionary process. If you do not have the ability to adapt to change, you will not survive the long haul. The trick is to keep what was good about the old traditions and blend them with new traditions.

Native Americans must develop an agenda that will result in a healing process for the country and all Native Americans. To meet the challenges of the future, Native Americans will need to develop a realistic three-tier ten-year agenda to take control of their destiny:

Individual Agenda

- ❖ Education, education, education…
- ❖ Get actively involved politically. Register and vote.
- ❖ Develop a positive physical image that includes confronting alcoholism and obesity. (Quit drinking alcohol as a way of life and eating frybread as a daily staple.)
- ❖ Nurture unique spirituality.
- ❖ Maintain cultural affiliation.

Tribal Agenda

- ❖ Focus on national Native American identity first and tribal affiliation second. Native Americans are one race of people with 559 tribes — not 559 different races.
- ❖ Forget archaic tribal animosities and prejudices that often date back hundreds of years. (They are ancient history and smack of tribal racism.)
- ❖ Establish progressive and definitive enrollment requirements. These requirements could include several status classifications with commensurate entitlements and

responsibilities. Who is and who isn't "Native American" must be redefined by current criteria that will result in a rational and equitable solution. Insidious forces are at work dividing Native Americans by various categories. The end result is that there are not enough people in any one category to be politically or economically significant.

❖ Aggressively solicit and expand tribal enrollment. Include everyone who meets tribal enrollment qualifications by issuance of a picture enrollment card. There are at least 15 million "wannabes" that are at-large potential Native American votes! Native American traditionalists must realize that in order to survive, they must embrace their urban brethren. It is not prudent for any group to exclude the largest segment (78%) of its constituency.

❖ Orchestrate a united tribal voting political coalition on the major Native American issues of health, education and entitlements.

❖ Establish a strategic geographic political agenda. In certain political arenas, a united Native American vote could be the deciding factor in important elections and issues. Every aspect of Native American life is determined by fickle political decisions. Native Americans live a precarious and fragile political existence.

National Agenda

❖ Develop a strategic campaign to marshal participants and resources. Analyze strengths and weaknesses.

❖ Initiate a national public relations campaign to penetrate the nation's conscience with a sustained multi-faceted professional approach.

❖ Utilize the above public relations campaign to solicit global community opinion and support by exposure of the Native American condition.

Who is and who isn't "Native American" must be redefined by current criteria that will result in a rational and equitable solution.

But that brief period of recrimination is over because the nation's conscience has been appeased by the attrition of time.

❖ Establish specific national concessions as retribution for past grievances.

❖ Establish national political unity to ensure those concessions are mandated.

❖ Develop a national coalition based on economic enterprise networking.

❖ Capitalize on the gaming window of opportunity to establish a basis for long-term social and economic development.

❖ The more successful casinos should contribute a small percentage to tribes with less resources and the Urban centers for the general entitlement and education of their relatives.

❖ Get involved with the Internet and the Native American Online portal.

Native Armageddon

For the last 100 years, the US Government initiated compensatory treaty entitlement programs because America took a look in the mirror and didn't like what it saw. But that brief period of recrimination is over because the nation's conscience has been appeased by the attrition of time.

Native tribes have "catch 22" dilemma. They are torn between trying to make the Federal government legally live up to its treaty trust responsibilities by funding social programs and at the same time declare themselves independent sovereign nations.

Native American people need to develop a military campaign mentality because tribal sovereignty and the reservation trust lands are essentially under siege. There are insidious forces at work in Congress today that would love to eliminate the reservation system.

The rationale will go something like this:

❖ The reservation system was an archaic idea in the first place and has been an injustice to the Native people. So let's correct the problem and abolish the system for their own good.

❖ Only 22% live on reservations. The vast majority have already left the reservations for education and employment opportunities.

❖ Reservation lands are not owned by the tribes; the lands are held in trust by the US Government for tribal use.

❖ The BIA money accounts debacle is too old, complex and expensive to resolve.

❖ The reservation allotment morass is too old, complex and costly to resolve.

❖ Native tribal programs already cost the taxpayers over $8 billion each year and are escalating.

❖ The government may need to confiscate the reservation mineral resources for the "common good," but tribal members will be justly compensated.

❖ Why should they be any more special than any other minority? Everyone took their turn in the barrel. The Africans, Chinese, Japanese, Hispanics, Irish, Italians, etc. all survived the "pecking order" of social integration.

❖ Many tribal governments are in chaos because of internal dissention and squabbling.

❖ The reservation system is over 100 years old and Native Americans are still the poorest race of people in the country with regard to health, education and welfare. Conclusive proof that the reservation system just doesn't work.

Urban Native Americans Migration

Year	Population	% Urban
1890	248,000	0.0
1900	237,000	0.4
1910	277,000	4.5
1920	244,000	6.1
1930	343,000	9.9
1940	345,000	7.2
1950	357,000	13
1960	524,000	28
1970	793,000	44
1980	1,364,000	49
1990	1,959,234	78
2000	2,400,000	??

There are 2.4 million Native Americans in the United States that has a population of 278 million. Approximately 22 percent of the 2.4 million live on reservations and the 78 percent majority live off reservation. Nationally, Native Americans are "out-marrying" at a rate of 70 percent. (Seven of 10 Native Americans do not marry other Native Americans.)

Ninety-eight percent of the Native American population are already tribally hyphenated (Chippewa-Ottawa-Sioux-Potawatami, etc.) and the majority are racially hyphenated (Chippewa-Ottawa-Irish-English, etc.).

Do the math and theoretically, in about two more generations, the vast majority of Native Americans who live off reservation will no longer be considered Native Americans because of blood quantum requirements.

If Native Americans can come to terms with the blood quantum issue, and get organized they will survive and even become stronger. If they do not, they will probably not survive as we know Native Americans today.

Native Americans that live on the reservations will survive tribal blood quantum requirements a few generations longer, but will eventually meet the same end result.

The composition of the national Native American community is like the widening concentric ripples when a stone is dropped in a pond:

❖ The center is the very small core group of Native people who live on the reservations, consider themselves to be full or nearly full-bloods, live traditionally, practice ceremonies and still speak their language.

❖ The 2nd circle are enrolled tribal members (estimated 1.4 million);

❖ The 3rd circle are people who consider themselves Native American and mark the Native American box on the Census 2000 form (estimated 1 million);

❖ The 4th circle is people who claim a Native American ancestor, but have become disconnected over the generations for a variety of reasons (some 15 million);

❖ And the 5th circle, and perhaps the largest, is people of conscience who are empathizers and sympathizers.

Native Americans must find a way to engage the support of that vast reservoir of people who claim Native American ancestry and those who are empathizers to a common cause, and still leave room for some avarice.

Tribal affiliation doesn't have to be either or, there can be degrees of recognition and benefits based on blood quantum or some other form of inequality. Most people outside of the two innermost circles, just want recognition and acknowledgement. (Which is their right.)

The Native people who live off-reservation and the Native people who live on reservation need each other. The two camps should complement each other, rather than be considered adversaries.

> *Tribal affiliation doesn't have to be either or, there can be degrees of recognition and benefits based on blood quantum or some other form of inequality.*

111

> *At less than 1 percent of the population, Native Americans will have to be a "tight" minority, politically and economically, in order to survive.*

Each of us bring our unique talents to the table and each of us has a job to do. I see no inconsistency between Urban Native American with their education, street smarts and business acumen working in concert with their Reservation counterparts that still have that precious spiritual, ceremonial and traditional connectivity. The reservations should be a welcome refuge where the exiled can rejuvenate their family and tribal connectivity.

Politics

As tribal and organization attorneys use the legal system to enforce entitlements, reparations and tribal sovereignty, a Native American political Armageddon is looming on the horizon. It's not a matter of if — it's a matter of when. At some point in the foreseeable future, the political issue will be the **national interest versus Native American interest.**

When the United States Congress decides that it is in the best interest of the nation to confiscate the mineral resources and/or to implement the "highest and best use" of land reserved exclusively for the use of a very small minority, it will happen. In a democracy, when the interest of a 99 percent majority is in direct conflict with a 1 percent minority, the majority will prevail. At less than 1 percent of the population, Native Americans will have to be a "tight" minority, politically and economically, in order to survive.

If necessary, clever lawyers will declare the treaties unconstitutional for one reason or another. There will be impassioned debates with a wailing and gnashing of teeth by Native tribes based on what is right, what is just and what is fair. However, when the dust settles, a Congressional committee (most of whom are totally ignorant about Native America) vote will be taken and the *organized* majority will prevail!

As anti-Native American forces mount and organize, Native Americans continue to bicker, squabble and quarrel among themselves, to the extent that they cannot present a united front within their own tribes, to say nothing of organizing 559 different tribes as a united voice. Civil disobedience is an option, but not a very good one. If Native America does not have a politically organized and well-funded defense strategy, they will lose!

Congress, the BIA and the anti-Native American establishment view this type of greedy, avaricious and inane behavior with great delight and further evidence that Native Americans are incapable of handling their own affairs.

Congress At Work

The Clinton impeachment hearings were a disturbing insight into the Congressional political process. At first blush, the issues were clear and a course of action seemed appropriate and inevitable. An immoral President got caught with his pants down in the Oval Office with a 22-year-old employee and then lied about a number of issues, under oath, to the American public. (We've heard the details ad nauseum.) His conduct was totally unacceptable and was condemned by everyone, especially the politicians. Republicans and Democrats alike, were publicly outraged and demanded immediate resignation for the *good of the country.*

Fast forward 6 months. The issue of right or wrong is completely obscured by the "spin" of clever lawyers, the media and politics. The bottom line is the decision — of whether or not to remove a President from office — was decided by a *political committee divided almost exactly down party lines.* This democratic decision supposedly reflects the "will" of the people and what is good for the country.

There are anti-Native American forces in Congress that advocate the dissolution of the reservation system as a means to confiscate reservation resources for the *"good of the country."* Based on the history of Native America, will this be the scenario in Congress?

The issue of right or wrong is completely obscured by the "spin" of clever lawyers, the media and politics.

113

The issue has always been the land and the problem has always been the lack of organization!

Window of Opportunity

A handful of the 559 tribes are enjoying gaming prosperity. For the first time in history, Native tribes have some resources and a window of opportunity to build a power base that could secure the future of all Native American people for generations to come.

3 factors make Native tribes a unique minority in this country:

❖ They were the Native inhabitants of this country;
❖ They have inherent tribal sovereignty and;
❖ They have a trust land base.

The issue has always been the land and the problem has always been the lack of organization! Native America has the talent, some political money and enough voters in certain parts of the country to impose their agenda on the political process and take control of their destiny.

What other race of people have the unprecedented opportunity to influence the course of their destiny, that Native America has? Will Native America rise to the occasion or will they self-destruct by blood quantum and internal political cannibalism?

If Native America could ever come together for a common cause, their collective voice would echo down the halls of Congress and into every committee hearing room. They could stage a demonstration that would make the "million man" march look like a walk in the park.

Notes:

_____

_____

_____

_____

_____

_____

_____

_____

_____

_____

_____

_____

Notes:

_____

_____

_____

_____

_____

_____

_____

_____

_____

_____

_____

_____

Native Americans have been mixing
inter-tribally for thousands of years
and inter-racially for at least 500 years.
Scientists at Howard University are
working on Mitochondrial DNA studies
which indicates that many more
millions of Americans than previously
thought probably have a Native
American ancestor.

Section 5:

Genealogy

The point is that because Native Americans have been mixing inter-tribally for thousands of years and interracially for 500 years, the chances are pretty good that untold millions of Americans probably have a Native American ancestor.

Do you have a Native American ancestor?

We get more inquiries related to genealogy than anything else. The inquiries usually go like this: "How do I go about establishing my Native American genealogy and become a tribal member?" I know that I had a great-great-great Native American ancestor, (I believe she was a Cherokee Princess) but older family members were vague or refused to talk about it."

Howard University researchers are using genetic testing methods to link millions of African-Americans to the part of Africa their ancestors hailed from. They have gotten positive results from African-Americans already tested and hope to market such a service by this summer. Marketing details will be worked out and the tests will be offered to the public in the price range of $200 to $300.

African-Americans descended from people brought here over a period of more than 350 years are not so African anymore. Tests have already revealed that about 30 percent of African males have a white male ancestor — often evidence one of their slave ancestors was the rape victim or mistress of a white plantation owner or overseer. Most African-Americans, no matter how dark their complexion, can claim at least one White or Native American ancestor, geneticists said.

The point is that because Native Americans have been mixing inter-tribally for thousands of years and interracially for 500 years, the chances are pretty good that untold millions of Americans probably have a Native American ancestor.

How can I become Tribally Enrolled?

Tribal enrollment criteria are set forth in tribal constitutions, articles of incorporation or ordinances. The criterion varies from tribe to tribe, so uniform membership requirements do not exist.

Two common requirements for membership are lineal descendancy from someone named on the tribe's base roll or relationship to a tribal member who descended from someone named on the base roll. (A "base roll" is the original list of members as designated in a tribal constitution or other document specifying enrollment criteria.) Other conditions such as tribal blood quantum, tribal residency, or continued contact with the tribe are common.

After you have completed your genealogical research, documented your ancestry, and determined which tribe with which your ancestor was affiliated, you are ready to contact the tribe directly to obtain the criteria for membership. Each tribe determines whether an individual is eligible for membership. Each tribe maintains it's own enrollment records and records about past members.

What are the Benefits and Services of Enrollment?

There has long been a myth that Native Americans receive a monthly check from the U.S. Government because of their status as Native Americans. There is no basis for this belief. Some tribes, tribal members and lineal descendants received payments from the Federal Government resulting from claims settlements. Very few judgment funds per capita payments remain today.

Some tribes distribute payments to enrolled members when revenues from the sale of tribal assets such as timber, hydroelectric power or oil and gas permit. Many tribes cannot make per capita payments because they do not have natural resources or other revenue from which they make a fund distribution.

There is a clear distinction between judgment funds and tribal funds. Judgment funds are appropriated by Congress after a claim that is filed by tribes or Native American descendant groups against the United States, is settled. Tribal funds are derived from tribal assets (refer to paragraph above). An individual does not have to be an enrolled member of a tribe to receive a final judgment fund payment. An individual must be an enrolled member of a tribe to be eligible to receive payments derived from tribal funds.

The BIA, through its government-to-government relationship with federally recognized tribes, carries out the Federal Government's unique and continuing relationship with and responsibility to tribes and Native American people. BIA programs support and assist federally recognized tribes in the development of tribal governments, strong economies, and quality programs. The scope of BIA programs is extensive and includes a range of services comparable to the programs of state and local government, e.g., education, social services, law enforcement, courts, real estate services, agriculture and range management, and resource protection.

Many Federal agencies other than the BIA have special programs to serve the American Native American population, i.e., the Native American Health Service (IHS), an adjunct of the Public Health Service, Department of Health and Human Services (DHHS). The IHS provides health care services through a network of reservation-based hospitals and clinics. Besides standard medical care, the agency has established programs that specialize in maternal and child health, mental health, substance abuse, home health care, nutrition, etc.

The Administration for Native Americans, another agency within DHHS, administers programs aimed at strengthening tribal governments and supporting the social and economic development of reservation communities. Other agencies of the Federal Government that serves the special needs of Native American people include the Departments of Housing and Urban Development, Justice, Agriculture, Education, Labor, Commerce and Energy.

All Native Americans, whether they live on or off reservations, are eligible (like all other citizens who meet eligibility requirements) to receive services provided by the state such as Temporary Assistance for Needy Families (TANF), Supplemental Security Income (SSI), the Food Stamp Program and the Low Income Heating and Energy Assistance Program (LIHEAP).

Contacting A Tribal Entity

The Bureau of Indian Affairs publishes a list of federally recognized Native American tribes in the *Federal Register.* The latest publication was on December 30, 1998, which can be obtained from most libraries, or accessed on the Internet. (See Internet address listings in the Bibliography.)

How do I begin my genealogy research?

The research of your "family tree" as a document for future generations is up to you.

The federal government does not do family research, nor does its National Archives collect or preserve family trees. Books on family history and genealogy are collected, complied, and published by private individuals who do so because they are interested descendants.

As the depository of the federal government's records deemed of permanent value for historical purposes, the National Archives houses many records that can be helpful to persons who wish to trace their ancestry. The search, however, cannot be completed at the National Archives alone. Many other depositories should be consulted. Following are suggestions about things to do and ways to go about getting a start at finding your ancestors:

The Internet

Our best advice is to explore and experiment with the tremendous explosion of genealogy resources on the Internet. A good place to start is Cyndi's List. (See Bibliography for web address.)

Computer Programs

There are a number of genealogy computer programs at your local computer store that will provide you with structure and format.

Start with Yourself

You are the trunk of your family tree and it branches out from you. Start with yourself, the known, and work toward the unknown.

You should find out all the vital information you can about your parents, write it down, then find out about your grandparents, great-grandparents, etc.

Names, Dates, Places, Relationships

You will be concerned with pulling from the many and varied documents of recorded history's four key items — names, places, dates, and relationships. These are the tools of the family researcher. People can be identified in records by their names, the dates of events in their lives (birth, marriage, death), the places they lived, and the relationships to others either stated or implied in the records.

Home Sources

The first place to begin is at home. You can find much information in family bibles, newspaper clippings, military certificates, birth and death certificates, marriage licenses, diaries, letters, scrapbooks, backs of pictures, baby books, etc.

Relatives as Source

Visit or write those in your family who may have information, particularly older relatives. More often than not, others before you have gathered data about the families in which you are interested. You should write a letter, make a personal visit, or conduct a telephone survey to find out about such persons and what information is already collected.

Finding Distant Relatives

Before launching your research program in libraries and archives, search for distant relatives who may have already performed research. Advertise in the local genealogical bulletins (city, county, or state) where your ancestors lived.

Birth, Marriage, and Death Records

Most states have a Department of Vital Records that keeps records of birth, deaths, marriages and divorces. Birth and death registration became a requirement around the turn of the century, about 1890–1915. Before that time these events will be found recorded generally in church records and family bibles. Marriages will be found recorded in most counties, dating often as early as the establishment of the county.

Church Records

Each Mormon Church of the Latter Day Saints has a Family History Center, usually staffed by volunteers, that is linked to the national archives in Salt Lake City. Mormons are one of the best and most competent genealogy resources available and they have a particular interest in Native American genealogy.

A few churches have records of important events in the lives of members but many do not. Investigate the possibility of finding genealogical data in the records of the church to which your ancestor belonged.

Deeds and Wills

Records of property acquisition and disposition can be good sources of genealogical data. Such records are normally in the county courthouses. Often the earliest county records or copies of them are also available in state archives.

Federal Records

The National Archives in Washington, D.C., has records of use in genealogical research. The federal census made every 10 years since 1790 is a good source. The census records are also available on microfilm in the National Archives' regional branches located in 11 metropolitan areas throughout the country (description leaflet available upon request). The National Archives also has military service and related records, passenger arrival records, and others. (See Bibliography for contact information.)

Libraries, Societies, Archives

Visit the state, regional, local institutions in your area. Libraries, historical and genealogical societies, and archival depositories are all good sources for genealogical and family history data.

Genealogy is Fun, Exciting & Rewarding

The detective work and research of Genealogy is an exciting and rewarding activity. Each person is entitled to acknowledgement of their ancestry.

Notes:

_____

_____

_____

_____

_____

_____

_____

_____

_____

_____

_____

_____

_____

_____

Notes:

_____

_____

_____

_____

_____

_____

_____

_____

_____

_____

_____

_____

The anthropology of the Native people of this country is a vast, complex and diverse subject. It would take a lifetime of study to understand their true place in history. The goal of Native American FAQ's and this Study Guide is to present enough information, direction and reference to motivate the reader to do further study and research in their area of interest.

Section 6:
Study Guide

Study Guidelines

This Study Guide format is fill-in blanks with essay questions that may be answered on a separate sheet of paper. All answers to all questions are found in *Native American FAQ's*.

This Study Guide can be downloaded and multiple copies printed for classroom use at: *www.nativeamericanonline.com/ studyguide*.

Population

The United States government's definition of a legal Indian:

> *Any person who has the certifiable Indian blood quantum to meet the enrollment requirements of a federally-recognized tribe.*

1. Census 2000 projects the Native American population at _____ million.

2. Of that population, approximately _____ million are tribally enrolled.

3. There are approximately _____ million people in the United States that have a discernible degree of Indian blood.

4. The total Indian population is less than _____ % of the total United States population.

5. Approximately _____ % of the Native American population live on reservations.

6. Approximately _____ % of the Native American population are urban Indians.

7. Do you think the urban Native American population will increase or decrease by 2050? (Explain your answer on a separate sheet of paper.)

8. Do you think the reservation Native American population will increase or decrease by 2050? (Explain your answer on a separate sheet of paper.)

9. Do you think the enrolled Native American population will increase or decrease by 2050? (Explain your answer on a separate sheet of paper.)

Tribes

The US government's definition for a federally-recognized tribe:

> *Any Indian tribe, band, nation, rancheria, pueblo, colony or community which is recognized by the United States government as eligible for the special programs and services provided by the Secretary of the Interior to Indians because of their status as Indians.*

1. There are _____ federally-recognized tribes in the United States.

2. There are approximately _____ state-recognized tribes.

3. Approximately _____ tribes are petitioning for federal recognition.

4. Each tribe has the right to determine the requirements for tribal _____ .

5. Certifiable _____ _____ is a basic requirement for tribal enrollment.

6. The _____ Nation of Oklahoma has the most enrolled members.

7. Approximately _____ % of Native Americans live on reservations?

8. Approximately _____ % of Native Americans live off reservation?

9. In your opinion, what is the future of Native American tribes as blood quantum is diluted through the natural process of inter-tribal and inter-racial assimilation? (Explain your answer on a separate sheet of paper.)

10. How could these tribes network politically and economically to achieve common goals? (Explain your answer on a separate sheet of paper.)

Reservations

A Federally-recognized Native American reservation is:

An area of land held in trust by the federal government reserved for Indian use.

1. There are _____ federally-recognized reservations in the United States.

2. These federally-recognized reservations are considered _____ nations.

3. These reservations occupy approximately _____ million acres.

4. Approximately _____ % are reservation trust lands.

5. Approximately _____ % are allotted lands.

6. The Department of _____ is the trustee of the US government.

7. The Bureau of _____ _____ (BIA) is responsible for the administration and management of the trust responsibilities.

8. The state of _____ has the most reservations.

9. The state of _____ has the largest reservation.

10. Approximately _____ % of the Native Americans live on reservations.

11. What is your understanding of Indian reservations as sovereign nations? (Explain your answer on a separate sheet of paper.)

Just the Facts

1. Native Americans were categorically granted US citizenship in (year) _____ .

2. Native Americans got the right to vote in Arizona in (year) _____ .

3. Native Americans got the right to vote in New Mexico in (year) _____ .

4. The United States is divided into a total of _____ BIA Regional Offices.

5. From 1778 to 1871, there were _____ treaties negotiated with Native tribes.

6. Approximately _____ tribes were relocated to Oklahoma Indian Territory during the 1800's.

7. The government spends $ _____ billion annually on Native American programs.

8. In your opinion, have Native Americans been socially and/or economically disadvantaged? (Explain your answer on a separate sheet of paper.)

Notes:

_____

_____

_____

_____

_____

_____

_____

_____

_____

_____

_____

_____

_____

The Internet has dramatically changed the way people do research. Most of the reports and lists used in the original edition of this book are no longer available in print. Most of the revisions and updated information for this printing are compiled from Internet websites.

Whenever possible, our website: **www.nativeamericanonline.com** is linked to sites than enhance or contain information that is relative.

S e c t i o n   7 :

Bibliography

■ Agency Contacts

BIA Regional Offices

Alaska Region
(Alaska)
P.O. Box 25520
Juneau, AK 99802
907-586-7177
Fax: 907-586-7169

Eastern Region
(Alabama, Florida, Connecticut, Louisiana, Maine, Mississippi, New York)
3701 N. Fairfax Drive
MS: 260-VASQ
Arlington, VA 22203
703-235-2571
Fax: 703-235-8610

Eastern Oklahoma Region
(Eastern Oklahoma)
101 North 5th St.
Muskogee, OK 74401-6206
918-687-2296
Fax: 918-687-2571

Great Plains Region
(Nebraska, North Dakota, South Dakota)
115 Fourth Ave., SE
Aberdeen, SD 57401-4384
605-226-7343
Fax: 605-226-7446

BIA Regional Offices (continued)

Midwest Region

(Michigan, Minnesota, Wisconsin, Iowa, Illinois)
One Federal Drive,
Room 550
Minneapolis, MN
55111-4007
612-713-4400
Fax: 612-713-4401

Navajo Region

(Arizona, New Mexico, Utah, Colorado)
P.O. Box 1060
Gallup, NM 87305
505-863-8314
Fax: 505-863-8324

Northwest Region

(Idaho, Oregon, Washington)
The Federal Building
911 NE, 11th Avenue
Portland, OR 97232
503-231-6702
Fax: 503-231-2201

Pacific Region

(California)
2800 Cottage Way
Sacramento, CA 95825
916-978-6000
Fax: 916-978-6099

Rocky Mountain Region

(Montana, Wyoming)
316 N. 26th Street
Billings, MT 59101
406-247-7943
Fax: 406-247-7976

BIA Regional Offices (continued)

Southern Plains Region
(Kansas, Texas, Western Oklahoma)
W.C.D. Office Complex
P. O. Box 368
Anadarko, OK 73005
405-247-6673
Fax: 405-247-2242

Southwest Region
(Colorado, New Mexico)
P.O. Box 26567
Albuquerque, NM
87125-6567
505-346-7590
Fax: 505-346-7517

Western Region
(Arizona, Nevada, Utah)
P. O. Box 10
Phoenix, AZ 85001
602-379-6600
Fax: 602-379-4413

State Indian Affairs Commissions

Alabama Indian Affairs Commission
669 S. Lawrence St.
Montgomery, AL 36104
334-242-2831

Arizona Commission of Indian Affairs
1400 W. Washington,
Suite 300
Phoenix, AZ 85007
602-542-3143
Fax 602-542-3223

California Indian Heritage Commission
915 Capitol Mall, Room 288
Sacramento, CA 95814
916-322-7791
Fax: 916-657-5390

Colorado Commission of Indian Affairs
130 State Capitol
Denver, CO 90203
303-866-3027
Fax: 303-866-5469

Connecticut Indian Affairs Council, DEP
165 Capitol Ave., Rm. 249
Hartford, CT 06106
860-238-3874

Florida Governor's Council on Indian Affairs
P.O. Box 10449
Tallahassee, FL 32302-2449
904-488-0730
Fax: 904-488-5875

State Indian Affairs Commissions (continued)

Hawaiian Homes Commission
P.O. Box 1879
Honolulu, HI 96805
808-586-3800
Fax: 808-586-3835

Iowa Governor's Council on Native Americans
100 1 North Dakota
Ames, IA 50010
515-292-0548
Fax: 515-239-1982

Maine Tribal State Relations Office
6 River Road
Indian Island, MI 04468
207-827-7776

Maryland Commission on Indian Affairs
100 Community Place
Crownsville, MD 21032-2023
410-514-7651
Fax: 410-987-4071

Massachusetts Commission on Indian Affairs
1 Ashburton Place,
Room 100 1
Boston, MA 01208
617-727-6394
Fax: 617-727-4938

Michigan Commission on Indian Affairs
611 W. Ottawa, 3rd Floor
Lansing, MI 48913
517-373-0654
Fax: 517-335-1642

State Indian Affairs Commissions (continued)

Minnesota Indian Affairs Council
1819 Bemidji Ave.
Bemidji, MN 56601
218-755-3825

Montana Governor's Office of Indian Affairs
State Capitol Building,
Room 202
Helena, MT 59620-0401
406-444-3702
Fax: 406-444-1350

Nebraska Indian Commission
P.O. Box 94981
Lincoln, NE 68509-4981
402-471-3475
Fax: 402-471-3392

Nevada Indian Affairs Commission
4600 Kietzke Lane,
Bldg B, Rm. 116
Reno. NV 89502
702-688-1347
Fax: 702-688-1803

New Jersey Commission on Indian Affairs
New Jersey Department of State
CN 300
Trenton, NJ 08625

New Mexico Office of Indian Affairs
224 East Palace Ave
Santa Fe, NM 87501
505-827-6440
Fax: 505-827-6445

State Indian Affairs Commissions (continued)

North Carolina Commission on Indian Affairs

325 N Salisbury St.,
Suite 579
Raleigh, NC 27603-5940
919-733-5998
Fax: 919-733-1207

North Dakota Indian Affairs Commission

600 E. Blvd., 1st Floor,
Judicial Wing
Bismarck, ND 58505
701-328-2428
Fax: 701-328-3000

Oklahoma Indian Affairs Commission

4545 N. Lincoln, Suite 282
Oklahoma City, OK 73105
405-521-3828
Fax: 405-521-0902

Oregon Commission on Indian Services

167 State Capitol
Salem, OR 97310
503-986-1067
Fax: 503-986-1071

South Dakota Office of Tribal Government Relations

118 W. Capitol,
Public Safety, Room 305
Pierre, SD 57501-2017
605-773-3415

Tennessee Commission on Indian Affairs

401 Church St.
Nashville, TN 37243-0459
615-532-0745

State Indian Affairs Commissions (continued)

Utah Division of Indian Affairs
324 S. State St., Suite 103
Salt Lake City, UT 84114
801-538-8808
Fax: 801-538-8803
Email: *cemain.wnumkena*
@state.ut.us

Virginia Council on Native Americans
202 N. 9th St., Suite 622
Richmond, VA 23219
804-786-7765
Fax: 804-371-6984

Washington Governor's Office of Indian Affairs
1515 S. Cherry St.,
P.O. Box 40909
Olympia, WA 98504-0909
360-753-2411
Email: *goiawa@aol.com*

Wyoming Native American Affairs Council
322 N. 8th St. West
Riverton, WY 82501
307-856-9828

State Indian Affairs Commissions (continued)

To our knowledge, the governors and legislatures in the following states have not created any official Native American Affairs offices, commissions, or council:

1. Alaska
2. Arkansas
3. Delaware
4. Georgia
5. Idaho
6. Illinois
7. Kansas
8. Kentucky
9. Louisiana
10. Mississippi
11. Missouri
12. New Hampshire
13. New York
14. Ohio
15. Pennsylvania
16. Rhode Island
17. South Carolina
18. Texas
19. Vermont
20. West Virginia
21. Wisconsin

■ Internet Resource Links

Most of the original research reports and lists used in earlier editions of this book are no longer available in print. The majority of the revisions and updated information for this printing are compiled from the Internet.

Native American Online
(*www.nativeamericanonline.com*)
    Reservation Roster
    Native American Reservations map
    Native American FAQ's Handbook

Bureau of Indian Affairs
(*www.doi.gov/bureau-indian-affairs.html*)
    Tribal Leaders List
    Federally-Recognized Tribes list
    List of Petitioning tribes
    Annual Report of Indian Lands

Genealogy
(*www.cyndislist.com*)

National Archives & Records Administration
(*www.nara.gov*)

Census Bureau
(*www.census.gov*)

Tribal Data Resources
(*www.tdronline.com*)

Native American Rights Fund
(*www.narf.org*)

American Indian Law Center
(*www.indianlaw.org*)

Native American Business Association
(*www.native-american-bus.org*)

Internet Resource Links (continued)

**National Center for American Indian
Enterprise Development**
(*www.ncaied.org*)

Indian Health Service
(*www.ihs.gov*)

National Indian Education Association
(*www.niea.org*)

National Congress of American Indians (*www.ncai.org*)

Vote Smart (*www.vote-smart.org*)

National Indian Gaming Commission (*www.nigc.gov*)

Native Indian Gaming Association (*www.indiangaming.org*)

Native American Publications:

Native People's Magazine (*www.nativepeoples.com*)

Indian Country Today (*www.indiancountry.com*)

News From Indian Country (*www.indiancountrynews.com*)

Catalogs of Native American Publications

American Indian Science & Engineering Society
(*www.aises.org*)

Four Winds Trading Company (*www.fourwinds-trading.com*)

Four Winds Indian Books (*www.fourwindsbooks.com*)

Native American Public Broadcasting Consortium
(*www.nativetelecom.org*)

Smithsonian Institution Press
(*www.si.edu/organiza/offices/sipress*)

The Falmouth Institute (*www.falmouthinst.com*)